Learning Words from Reading

Also available from Bloomsbury

Acquiring Metaphorical Expressions in a Second Language,
by Chris Mengying Xia
Language Acquisition and the Multilingual Ideal,
by Toshiyuki Nakamura
Study Abroad and the Second Language Learner,
edited by Martin Howard
Teaching Pragmatics and Instructed Second Language Learning,
by Nicola Halenko
The Production-Comprehension Interface in Second Language Acquisition,
by Anke Lenzing

Learning Words from Reading

*A Cognitive Model of
Word-Meaning Inference*

Megumi Hamada

BLOOMSBURY ACADEMIC
LONDON • NEW YORK • OXFORD • NEW DELHI • SYDNEY

BLOOMSBURY ACADEMIC
Bloomsbury Publishing Plc
50 Bedford Square, London, WC1B 3DP, UK
1385 Broadway, New York, NY 10018, USA
29 Earlsfort Terrace, Dublin 2, Ireland

BLOOMSBURY, BLOOMSBURY ACADEMIC and the Diana logo are trademarks of
Bloomsbury Publishing Plc

First published in Great Britain 2021
Paperback edition published in 2023

Copyright © Megumi Hamada, 2021

Megumi Hamada has asserted her right under the Copyright, Designs and Patents Act,
1988, to be identified as Author of this work.

All rights reserved. No part of this publication may be reproduced or transmitted in
any form or by any means, electronic or mechanical, including photocopying, recording,
or any information storage or retrieval system, without prior permission in writing from
the publishers.

Bloomsbury Publishing Plc does not have any control over, or responsibility for,
any third-party websites referred to or in this book. All internet addresses given in this
book were correct at the time of going to press. The author and publisher regret any
inconvenience caused if addresses have changed or sites have ceased to exist,
but can accept no responsibility for any such changes.

A catalogue record for this book is available from the British Library.

A catalog record for this book is available from the Library of Congress.

ISBN: HB: 978-1-3501-5367-7
PB: 978-1-3502-5170-0
ePDF: 978-1-3501-5368-4
eBook: 978-1-3501-5369-1

Typeset by Deanta Global Publishing Service, Chennai, India

To find out more about our authors and books visit www.bloomsbury.com and sign up for
our newsletters.

Contents

List of Figures — vi
Preface — vii

Part I What Do We Know about Incidental Word Learning from Reading?

1 Theoretical Background of Word Learning from Reading — 3
2 Mechanism of Word Learning from Reading — 11
3 Factors in Word Learning from Reading — 28

Part II How Do We Obtain Information from Reading and Use It for Word-Meaning Inference?

4 Introducing the Cognitive Model of Word-Meaning Inference — 45
5 Extracting Word-Form Information — 63
6 Generating Contextual Information — 83
7 Pedagogical Applications — 108

References — 127
Index — 156

Figures

4.1	Cognitive model of word-meaning inference	57
5.1	Characteristics of writing systems	66
6.1	Example of the minimum attachment principle	87
6.2	Example of the late closure principle	88
6.3	Mental representation of the butterfly, lily pad, and tadpole	94
7.1	Sample sentence anagram task	116

Preface

I would first like to explain what motivated me to write a book about reading and vocabulary. Vocabulary is undoubtedly the most difficult aspect of learning a language. Just like most language learners, I myself experienced the difficulty of learning words. My formal L2 instruction (English) started in the seventh grade in Japan. There were some words that my teachers provided explicit instruction for, but as I moved up to higher grades, classroom instruction never mentioned individual words. Vocabulary was something that we as students had to work on by ourselves, somehow. There was a book of words that appeared in standardized tests, and we tried to learn them all. I remember I started learning (or memorizing) the letter *a* section in the book, using various self-learning techniques, such as reciting them, writing down the words and their L1 translations many times, and quizzing myself (covering up the L1 translations and seeing if I could say the meanings). I had to keep trying little by little every day as much as I could. Of course, it was extremely hard to learn all of the words in the book, and I never finished going over all of them. My memory of vocabulary learning was that it was very painful and boring. I suspect that your memory is similar to mine. I wished there was an easier way to learn words. When I began my research career in Applied Linguistics and Second Language Acquisition, I wanted to find a way to help ease the burden of vocabulary learning.

During my time as a graduate student, I began my research career in the psycholinguistics of reading, motivated by my professors and fellow graduate students at Carnegie Mellon and the University of Pittsburgh. I was fascinated by learning about how our minds work when we see printed words, how we comprehend messages from a text, and how these processes vary across languages. I began seeing vocabulary learning from a perspective slightly different from when I initially had become interested in the topic. I continued learning about various vocabulary studies by many great researchers and came across Paul Meara's article (Meara, 1997) calling for the need for collaboration or rapprochement between (applied) linguists and psycholinguists, both of whom work on vocabulary, but approach it from different traditions. There have been a number of collaborations since then, but there is still a need in the areas of reading and vocabulary. This is the reason why I pursued this book project.

One of the difficulties of word learning is that there are so many words that we have to learn in order to be able to use a language to an adequate degree. As you will see in this book, some estimates say as many as 8,000–9,000 word families are necessary for comprehending authentic material. In addition to words that are in dictionaries, there are new words constantly being created. Incidental word learning, the focus of the first half of the book, is assumed to help alleviate the burden of learning so many words. For example, you can learn new words from reading novels or magazines for the purpose of reading, not for the purpose of word learning. However, there are concerns about whether incidental word learning is a method that benefits all students, despite studies suggesting its effectiveness.

This book aims to advance the understanding of incidental word learning from reading by introducing relevant theories and models in the psycholinguistics of reading. The book consists of two parts. The first part, "What Do We Know about Incidental Word Learning from Reading?," provides a summary of the studies on the topic of vocabulary and reading, mainly from the applied linguistics field. The second part, "How Do We Obtain Information from Reading and Use It for Word-Meaning Inference?," describes the theories and findings from the psycholinguistics field, including word recognition, sentence processing, and reading comprehension, and proposes the model, the Cognitive Model of Word-Meaning Inference, which illustrates how the meanings of words encountered during reading are learned (or inferred). As cross-linguistic transfer affects reading processes, the second part also addresses possible cross-linguistic transfer in word-meaning inference. It is hoped that this book will lead either directly or indirectly to the improvement of vocabulary learning and teaching approaches.

Part I

What Do We Know about Incidental Word Learning from Reading?

1

Theoretical Background of Word Learning from Reading

How many words do you know in your native language? How many words do you know in your non-native language? If you are reading this book, you probably know so many words that you cannot even count or keep track of how many. The next question to think about is how you learned the words. Do you still remember how you learned some of the words? As you know, there are many ways to learn words, such as classroom instruction, memorization techniques, consulting a dictionary, watching a movie, or asking someone for help, just to name a few. This book addresses word learning from reading. Have you experienced learning new words while reading even though you did not plan to learn them? Here is one way to describe the phenomenon of word learning from reading. You are reading a book and see an unfamiliar word. The word appears multiple times. You start guessing the meaning of it based on the context surrounding the word. As an introduction, this chapter provides an overview of the theoretical and historical background of the research that has established the notion that students learn words from reading.

1.1 Origin of the Incidental Learning Hypothesis

Students learn new words from reading. This claim is referred to as the default learning hypothesis (e.g., Jenkins and Dixon, 1983) or the incidental learning hypothesis (Webb and Nation, 2017). The notion that students are able to learn new words from reading initially emerged among researchers and teachers in L1 settings because it provided a reasonable explanation for the massive growth of word knowledge in grade school. According to Jenkins and

Dixon (1983), a conservative estimate of word knowledge based on Dupuy (1974) indicates that typical children know about 2,000 words at Grade 3 and 5,000 words at Grade 7, demonstrating that there is an increase of nearly 3,000 words in just a few years. How do children manage to learn so many words in a relatively short period of time?

Jenkins and Dixon (1983) argued that it would be unrealistic to assume that the children learned all these words through classroom instruction. They certainly learned some words through instruction, but it would simply not be possible for teachers to provide explicit instruction on all of the words. Thus, the only possible explanation for the massive growth of word knowledge was that they must have learned most of the words on their own through a naturalistic method. This explanation coincided with a general belief among teachers. Vocabulary should not be directly taught. It should be learned naturally. Reading seemed to provide a perfect condition for word learning because children were exposed to an enormous amount of words through reading on a daily basis. Upon the arrival of empirical evidence, suggesting that children were able to learn new words from reading (e.g., Jenkins, Stein, and Wysocki, 1984; Nagy, Herman, and Anderson, 1985), the default learning hypothesis became widely accepted in L1 reading research and instruction.

1.2 Incidental Learning Hypothesis in Second Language

1.2.1 Theoretical Background of the Incidental Learning Hypothesis

In the 1950s and 1960s, the theoretical approach prevalent in L2 learning was behaviorism. Under the behavioristic approach (Skinner, 1957), language learning was considered to be the same as learning any other skill (e.g., driving a car). It was believed that learning occurred as a result of habit formation, generated by patterns of stimulus-response with reinforcement. In the classroom, students were expected to respond to specific situations, and they received reinforcement when they responded correctly. For instance, learning how to order at a restaurant, the students would be trained to respond to an utterance by a server, "Can I take your order?" by responding, "I would like a sandwich." When they became fluent in responding to the utterance, they would respond using different items, such as "I would like a coffee, I would like a salad." Repetition and drills were the primary techniques in teaching these exchanges.

In the 1970s, the behavioristic approach was challenged by the theories of cognitive psychologists and linguists (e.g., Chomsky, 1959; Slobin, 1970), who focused on understanding the cognitive processes involved in learning and using language. Based on data from children's L1 development, the researchers suggested that language acquisition or language development occurred naturally in all humans. Language was not only what we observed through writing or speaking, but language was also a mental representation in our thought processes. Even very young children who had not yet started speaking sentences exhibited knowledge of the language used in the environment they were immersed in.

Following the cognitive approaches, in the late 1970s through the 1980s, Krashen proposed one of the most influential models in L2 acquisition, the monitor model, which encompassed the following hypotheses: the acquisition-learning hypothesis, the monitor hypothesis, the natural order hypothesis, the input hypothesis, and the affective filter hypothesis (Krashen, 1981, 1982, 1985). These hypotheses were formed based on the assumption that L2 learning was most effective when it occurred naturally, in a way similar to a child learning their native language.

Among Krashen's hypotheses, the input hypothesis is the one that offered theoretical support for incidental word learning from reading (see Krashen, 1989). The hypothesis assumes that L2 learners acquire language through comprehensible input, which is defined as "$i + 1$." The "i" refers to the learners' current language ability, and "$+ 1$" refers to an amount of new material that is challenging but provides an opportunity to learn something new. In other words, the input needs to be neither too easy nor too difficult, but should be slightly challenging for the learners, by exposing them to a limited amount of unfamiliar material. Just like L1 children, L2 learners are exposed to many words through reading, including both familiar and unfamiliar words. Reading is considered to be the ideal medium for providing comprehensible input for word learning.

1.2.2 What Is Incidental Word Learning?

Incidental word learning is most commonly defined as word learning that occurs as a by-product of a main cognitive activity involving comprehension through listening and/or reading (Gass, 1999). For example, you are watching a movie or reading a novel for pleasure. You are not trying to learn new words, but you happen to learn a new word by guessing its meaning from the context.

Incidental word learning is often contrasted with intentional word learning. According to Hulstijn (2003), intentional learning refers to a method of learning through specific attention to words (e.g., learning with various memory aids) and is restricted to the learning of factual knowledge (e.g., a word's definition). On the other hand, incidental learning refers to a method of learning through reading and listening and can be used for the learning of both factual and abstract knowledge. The word, "incidental," may be understood as "unconscious," but this is clearly not the case. Schmidt (1994) states that attention to and noticing of language are involved in all forms of learning, even in incidental learning. In incidental learning, the object of learning is not words, but something else (e.g., learning grammar, learning about history), but learners still pay attention to the language they are engaged in.

Huckin and Coady (1999) argue that incidental word learning from reading offers unique advantages. Because students encounter unfamiliar words in context, they are able to learn a richer sense of the meanings and usages of the words more effectively than learning through a traditional method (e.g., paired-associative learning). Also, incidental word learning is more individualized. Students gain word knowledge through reading texts of their own choice, as much of word learning is expected to occur through some form of self-learning, rather than classroom instruction. Furthermore, incidental word learning from reading is pedagogically efficient because it enables two learning goals (word learning and reading) to occur at the same time.

Nevertheless, despite the popularity of incidental word learning, there are some concerns as to whether it is reasonable to assume that all learners can take advantage of the method. Laufer (2005, 2010) points out that the incidental learning hypothesis is based on a set of assumptions: learners are able to notice unfamiliar words in a text, infer the meanings of the words correctly, and remember the meanings they inferred; and there is enough contextual information in the text to enable word-meaning inference. Obviously, it is too optimistic to think that learners are always able to meet all of these assumptions. Laufer (2005, 2010) suggests that word-focused instruction needs to accompany reading because comprehensible input from reading alone is insufficient for word learning, extending the research on focus on form and focus on formS in grammar instruction (e.g., Doughty, 2003; Long, 1991) to word learning.

1.2.3 What Is Lexical Inference?

Let us first take a look at the following set of sentences. Based on the sentences provided, what do you think the meaning of the target pseudoword, *gend*, is?

1. It is nice to visit a gend on a sunny day.
2. We moved to this house because there are many gends nearby.
3. My friend said, "Let's have a picnic at the gend near the river tomorrow."
4. It seems there are some wild animals living in this gend.
5. The children loved running around in the gend.
6. There is an outdoor concert this coming weekend at the gend.

The meaning of *gend* is "park." In each sentence, you probably were able to make an informed guess about possible meanings of the word. You might have guessed that it is probably a noun and means something positive, rather than negative.

The term, *inferencing*, was first introduced by Carton (1971), who applied the thinking processes involved in solving a cloze test, such as the example mentioned earlier, to the context of word learning from reading. He explains that three types of cues are used in lexical inferencing: intra-lingual, inter-lingual, and extra-lingual cues. The intra-lingual cues are morpho-syntactic cues, such as prefixes and suffixes (e.g., "don*ation*"), plural markers, grammatical gender, or animate/inanimate status of the word's meaning. The inter-lingual cues refer to similarities between L1 and L2 that learners can make use of when they infer the meaning of unfamiliar words. The extra-lingual cues are contextual cues that learners derive from a given text. Since the Carton study, numerous studies have been published on the topic of lexical inference. Studies on this topic are typically concerned with the factors and processes involved in the meaning inference of unfamiliar words during reading (see Chapter 3 for more details).

Haastrup (1991: 40) defines lexical inference as "making informed guesses as to the meaning of a word in light of all available linguistic cues in combination with the learner's general knowledge of the world and awareness of context." Because lexical inference refers specifically to the inference of word meanings, the term, word-meaning inference, is used hereafter in this book. It is important to clarify the difference between "word-meaning inference" and "incidental word learning" because they sometimes refer to the same learning phenomenon, depending on how studies define incidental word learning. In this book, the two terms refer to different learning phenomena. Word-meaning inference refers only to the process involved in guessing of a word's meaning from reading. On the other hand, incidental word learning is an umbrella term that refers to all processes involved in word learning, including different aspects of words (e.g., meaning, spelling, pronunciation) as well as retention of the learned words. Word-meaning inference is one method or technique for learning word meanings.

1.2.4 Incidental Learning Hypothesis and Reading Instruction

Extensive reading is an instructional program that promotes incidental word learning from reading. In an extensive reading program, L2 learners read large quantities of material that are within their linguistic competence (Grabe and Stoller, 2011). The learners are expected to gain word knowledge incidentally through reading book-length materials for an extended period of time. Extensive reading originates from the reading programs for native-speaking children, such as (uninterrupted) sustained silent reading (SSR), free voluntary reading, pleasure reading, book flood, independent reading, and Drop Everything And Read (DEAR). These programs have been widely implemented in grade schools and continue to receive support from both L1 literacy researchers and teachers (e.g., Garan and DeVoogd, 2008; Lee-Daniels and Murray, 2000; Picarello, 1986; Stahl, 2004).

Extensive reading has also been shown to be effective for promoting L2 reading development (Day and Bamford, 1998; Krashen, 1993; Nakanishi, 2015; Pilgreen, 2000; Stoller, 2015; Yamashita, 2015). More specifically, studies have suggested that extensive reading contributes to the development of reading fluency (Greenberg et al., 2006; Huffman, 2014), reading comprehension and vocabulary (Suk, 2016), and motivation for reading and establishing a reading habit (Lee, 2011; Rodrigo, Greenberg, and Segal, 2014).

L2 studies have demonstrated that extensive reading promotes incidental word learning (e.g., Elley and Mangubhai, 1983; Horst, Cobb, and Meara, 1998; Horst, 2005). For example, in a study with Fijian ESL children, Elley and Mangubhai (1983) found that the children who spent twenty to thirty minutes each day in SSR with books of their own choice improved L2 skills, including vocabulary. Chapter 2 offers more details on extensive reading. Extending the concepts of extensive reading, more recent findings suggest that repeated reading and assisted-repeated reading (with the aid of an audio-reading) enhance reading comprehension as well as incidental word learning (e.g., Han and Chen, 2010; Webb and Chang, 2012). Refer to Chapter 3 for more details on this topic.

In implementing an extensive reading program, there are some principles that should be kept in mind, in addition to having students read a lot of materials. According to Day and Bamford (2002), in an extensive reading program, students should choose the materials they want to read, and the purpose of reading should be for pleasure (e.g., learning about new topics, such as travel or technology), rather than practicing language skills. They should read easy materials on a wide range of topics silently on their own with reasonable speed, rather than slowly. The teacher's role is to guide the students as well as to be a role model as an engaged reader. Therefore, the teacher should also be participating in extensive reading.

It has been recommended that extensive reading be incorporated into a language course, because extensive reading provides a condition ideal for word learning (see Nation, 2015). This is because in extensive reading, students focus on the message being communicated, instead of the individual words and phrases, and have opportunities to encounter the same word multiple times in different contexts. Nation and Waring (2020) provide guidelines for incorporating an extensive reading program into a language course. They recommend that the following four strands be included in the course: meaning-focused input (comprehending messages and incidental word learning), meaning-focused output (communicating messages through speaking and writing), language-focused learning (intentional word learning), and fluency development (reading easy and familiar materials).

1.3 Chapter Summary

Reading and vocabulary are interrelated. Vocabulary knowledge is probably the most important knowledge in the development of reading ability. Nevertheless, vocabulary is probably the most difficult knowledge to develop because there is an enormous number of words that students need to learn. No class would be able to teach every word to students, yet they are somehow able to develop a massive amount of word knowledge. How do they develop word knowledge? According to the default learning hypothesis (e.g., Jenkins and Dixon, 1983) or the incidental learning hypothesis (Webb and Nation, 2017), students learn new words incidentally through reading. The incidental learning hypothesis argues that students can learn words from reading, by inferring the meanings of new words from context. Instruction based on the hypothesis has been implemented through extensive reading programs, which incorporate a vocabulary component into reading instruction. The students are expected to learn new words incidentally from reading, and as they read more, they are expected to learn more words. The incidental learning method has become a popular approach in vocabulary instruction, but there is concern about the effectiveness of the method (Laufer, 2005, 2010). In order to provide a more comprehensive understanding of the method, the next two chapters detail the mechanisms and factors in word learning from reading.

2

Mechanism of Word Learning from Reading

In this chapter, we are going to look into how word learning from reading occurs. To understand the mechanism of the learning processes, it is necessary to clarify what it means to know a word. The first section of the chapter explains the nature of word knowledge, by introducing aspects and dimensions of word knowledge. The second section summarizes the frameworks in word learning from reading that are currently available. The frameworks describe the processes or steps involved in learning words encountered during reading. The last section summarizes the effectiveness of incidental word learning from reading. Although students can learn new words incidentally from reading, it is still unclear how effective it is as a method of vocabulary instruction. The section highlights some of the findings from incidental word learning as well as findings from studies that compared the incidental method to the intentional method.

2.1 Nature of Word Knowledge

2.1.1 Aspects of Word Knowledge

Do you know the word, *swift*? If you answered "yes," what is the reason for saying that you know the word? Generally, we say we know a word when we know the meaning of the word. That is, when we are presented with the word, either in spoken or written form, we are able to identify the meaning attached to the word. For *swift*, you probably thought of meanings such as "fast and quick." The word also refers to a type of small bird that can fly very fast. If you thought of only the first meaning (fast and quick) but did not know the other meaning, would you still say that you "know" the word? If you can identify the meanings of *swift* when reading or listening but you are not able to use it when writing or speaking, would you still say you "know" the word? As shown in the example, our assessment of knowing may vary depending on how we define word knowledge. The definitions are complex in nature because word knowledge involves multiple dimensions (Henriksen, 1999).

Nation's (2001) definition of word knowledge is one that has been frequently referred to in L2 research. In the definition, word knowledge entails three major aspects, form, meaning, and use. Word form refers to the visual (how it's written) or spoken (how it's pronounced) label of a word. Word form also includes word parts within a word. For example, *rework* includes a prefix, *re-*, and a root, *work*, and *bookcase* includes two roots, *book* and *case*. Word meaning refers to the meaning that a word form signals, also including concept and referents and the associations with other words. Word use refers to grammatical function, collocation (words or types of words it occurs with), and constraints on use. In addition, the definition includes receptive skills (listening and reading) and productive skills (speaking and writing) for each of the aspects. For example, being able to recognize a word form in reading and being able to spell it are two separate aspects of word knowledge.

2.1.2 Breadth and Depth of Word Knowledge

Nagy and Herman (1987) explain that there are two dimensions in word knowledge: breadth and depth. Breadth of word knowledge refers to the size, namely, how many words one knows. If we know at least one meaning of a word, we normally count it as a "known" word. Using the example of *swift* mentioned earlier, the most common meaning is probably "fast and quick." If we know this particular meaning, we tend to count this word as a "known" word, even though we do not know another meaning, "a type of small bird that can fly very fast." In contrast, depth of word knowledge refers to how much the learners know about a word. Therefore, knowing both meanings of *swift* demonstrates more knowledge than knowing only one of them. In addition to knowledge of word meaning, depth of knowledge also includes all the other aspects of word knowledge included in Nation's definition.

Even though both breadth and depth are equally important, breadth is typically the dimension used for testing students' word knowledge. The vocabulary knowledge scale (Wesche and Paribakht, 1996) is a tool that enables assessment of word knowledge in more detail. It includes the following five degrees: (1) unfamiliar with the word; (2) familiar with the form but unfamiliar with the meaning; (3) familiar with the form and know a likely meaning; (4) familiar with the form and the meaning; (5) can use the word in a sentence. For each word to be assessed, learners evaluate their own knowledge and indicate which scale degree their knowledge is at.

2.1.3 Partial Word Knowledge

Another important factor to consider in defining word knowledge is that word knowledge is incremental in nature. Durso and Shore (1991) classified word knowledge into three levels: known, frontier, and unknown. Words that belong to the known level were the words whose meanings could be stated, and words that belong to the frontier level were the words that were considered vaguely familiar, indicating partial word knowledge. In their study, English L1 college students were asked to judge whether low-frequency target words (e.g., *dowager*) were used correctly in a sentence. Overall, the researchers found that the students performed better in the sentence decision task when the target word was a word they previously identified as frontier, compared to a word that was identified as unknown. The findings were confirmed in the subsequent studies (Lockett and Shore, 2003; Shore and Kempe, 1999), suggesting that word knowledge involves a frontier level and that partial knowledge consists of the knowledge of what a word does *not* mean, rather than what a word means.

The instructional implications of partial word knowledge are somewhat mixed. For example, in a study with native speakers (Grades 4–6 and college students), Adolf et al. (2016) suggested that repeated exposures to a target word in a high-quality sentence context were more important than having partial knowledge. Comparing two groups of ESL learners (intermediate and advanced levels) to native speakers, Zareva (2012) pointed out that the greatest problem with the frontier words for intermediate-level learners was overestimating their knowledge, that is, they misjudged that they knew a word that they actually did not know.

2.1.4 Word Knowledge Development in Reading

Coady (1993, 1997) suggests that the words that learners encounter while reading can be categorized into the following three developmental stages: unfamiliar, somewhat familiar when it's in a context, and familiar and recognized automatically irrespective of the context. Needless to say, the words in the first stage (unfamiliar) create difficulty in reading comprehension. Learners are expected to either infer the meanings of the unfamiliar words from the context, or look them up in a dictionary, or leave them uncomprehended.

Coady (1997) also stresses the importance of basic word knowledge in inferring the meanings of unknown words from reading. If a majority of the words the learners encounter are not in the third stage of development (familiar and recognized automatically), it is not possible for them to accurately infer the meanings of unfamiliar words because they are not able to generate sufficient clues from the text they are reading. He also points out that more experienced readers are better able to infer the meanings of unknown words from reading. Pulido and Hambrick (2008) offer the data to support this claim, demonstrating relationships between expertise in reading, sight vocabulary, reading comprehension, and L2 vocabulary growth.

2.2 Frameworks in Word Learning from Reading

2.2.1 What Do Learners Do When They Encounter Unknown Words during Reading?

Earlier research that introduced the idea of word learning from reading was mainly concerned with how learners would deal with unknown words they encountered during reading. The ways in which they would treat the unknown words were referred to as strategies, and attempting to infer the words' meanings was one of the strategies. For example, Fraser (1999) investigated the use of three strategies (ignore, consult, and infer) with college-level ESL students who were at the intermediate level of proficiency. The ignore strategy referred to when the students did nothing about unknown words they encountered during reading. The consult strategy referred to when they looked up the meanings of the unknown words using some kind of aid (e.g., a dictionary). The infer strategy referred to when they inferred the meanings based on the linguistic information available in the text.

Over five months, the students read texts and provided explanations as to how they had dealt with the words using a retrospective think-aloud technique, which is a common way of measuring an individual's cognitive processes (Ericsson and Simon, 1984). The results from strategy frequency indicated that consult was used 29 percent of the time, ignore was used 24 percent of the time, infer was used 44 percent of the time, and no attention was used 3 percent of the time. When they consulted or inferred alone, the students retained the learned words' meanings 30 percent and 31 percent of the time, respectively. These findings demonstrated the potential for using word-meaning inference as a vocabulary learning method.

Similarly, Paribakht and Wesche (1999) investigated how college-level ESL students who were at the intermediate level of proficiency would deal with unknown words encountered during reading, using the think-aloud technique. The researchers found that more than half of the unknown words were ignored, but word-meaning inference was the most common strategy for the words that were not ignored. They concluded that word-meaning inference involved more conscious effort during input processing, in which the students integrated multiple knowledge sources, such as grammar, word morphology, and world knowledge. Additionally, they pointed out that it would be beneficial to use tasks that accompany reading to facilitate input processing.

2.2.2 Input Processing

There is an area of research that investigates how learners process input from a text when they learn words from reading. The primary interest is finding and defining ways to engage learners in a deeper level of input processing, based on the depth of processing hypothesis (Craik and Lockhart, 1972), which contends that deeper levels of cognitive processing lead to better learning outcome, defined as retention. What does a "deeper level" of cognitive processing entail in learning words from reading? There are several definitions offered by researchers. For instance, Joe (1995) claims that the following three processes are involved: attention (attending to various aspects of a word, such as word form), retrieval (using the learned words in meaningful contexts), and generation (constructing novel ways of using target words in new contexts). Paribakht and Wesche

(1996) suggest that the following five processes are involved: selective attention, recognition, manipulation, interpretation, and production.

More recently, Ender (2016) suggests that successful word learning from reading involves both implicit and explicit processing of input provided by a text, based on think-aloud data from college students learning French. The levels of processing involved are an implicit process of choosing a target word, a conscious decision to determine the meaning of the word, and further analysis of the text input. In processing the input, what is considered important is the connection between word form and word meaning. The data showed that the learners made use of word-form information to determine the meaning of the word, and then checked it against the context.

The involvement load hypothesis (Hulstijn and Laufer, 2001; Laufer and Hulstijn, 2001) proposes that three components, need, search, and evaluation, are entailed in learning words from reading. The need component is concerned with the need to achieve or gain new knowledge, in other words, a motivational factor. Unless there is a need, a learner would not attempt to infer the meanings of unknown words but would probably ignore them instead. The search and evaluation components are concerned with cognitive processes, referring to a process of searching for the meanings of unknown words and a process of verifying whether the meanings fit their contexts, respectively. The hypothesis also states that words whose information is processed with higher involvement load are retained better than words processed with lower involvement load. Thus, reading-related tasks with a higher involvement load are more effective for retaining the knowledge of words learned (or inferred) than tasks with a lower involvement load. L2 studies have also investigated the effectiveness of reading and reading-related tasks in word learning from reading (e.g., Peters et al., 2009). The findings are uniformly supportive of the hypothesis, claiming that tasks that involve a deeper level of cognitive processing lead to better retention of the learned words (the meaning and/or form of the words). See Chapter 3 for more detailed explanation about tasks that accompany reading.

2.2.3 Word-Meaning Inference Processing

There are a few models that detail the processes involved in word-meaning inference. One such model, the Haastrup model (1991), describes word-meaning inference as a process of hypothesis formation and testing. The hypothesis is formed based on the input that learners receive, including the following three sources: input outside educational situation, learners' existing linguistic knowledge (L1 and L2), and input inside educational situation (available in the text). The learners form a hypothesized meaning of an unfamiliar word based on these inputs and test the hypothesis by checking to see if it fits in the context. If the hypothesis testing turns out positive, the hypothesized meaning becomes part of their word knowledge. If the testing turns out negative, they reconstruct a new hypothesis.

De Bot, Paribakht, and Wesche (1997) developed a lexical processing model, based on Levelt's speech production model (1989). The lexical processing model includes two paths: comprehension and production. The comprehension path describes how word knowledge is formed through the input learners receive, and the production path describes how word knowledge is accessed and used for language production. Both paths go through three levels of mental representation, which are the conceptual, the lemma, and the lexeme levels. Concept is similar to lexicon in Levelt's model, which refers to the knowledge of a word. Lemma refers to the knowledge of semantic and syntactic (e.g., part of speech) aspects of a word, and lexeme refers to the knowledge of word form. In inferring the meaning of an unknown word, the lexeme is provided in the text. Learners first need to identify whether they know the word, that is, whether they possess the semantic aspect of lemma (the meaning of the word) for a given lexeme in their mental lexicon. If they determine that they do not know the meaning of the word, they proceed to work on figuring out meaning (the semantic lemma), by inferring the meaning of the word.

Huckin and Block's (1993) model is a framework that incorporates the processes involved in reading and word-meaning inference in a more comprehensive manner. Similar to Haastrup (1991), this model views word-meaning inference as hypothesis generation and testing. The knowledge sources that lead to the construction of vocabulary knowledge include text schemata, syntax and morphology, world knowledge (e.g., topic knowledge), text representation, and permanent memory. If learners determine that they have sufficient knowledge to infer the meanings of unknown words, they proceed to generate hypothesized meanings and test whether the hypotheses are correct. Although this model identifies several different knowledge sources, learners may not use all of the sources before they proceed to generate the hypothesized meanings. For example, Huckin and Block (1993) reported that college-level

ESL students used only the word parts (morphological information) to infer the meanings of unknown words. They then used contextual information to evaluate whether the hypothesized meanings made sense in the surrounding context.

2.2.4 Contextual Processing

The framework proposed by Sternberg and Powell (1983) is based on literacy research conducted with English L1 children. Focusing on how contextual information is processed, the framework describes three stages that are involved in word-meaning inference: selective encoding, selective combination, and selective comparison. Selective encoding refers to the process of separating relevant from irrelevant information for the purpose of formulating a definition. Selective combination refers to the process of combining relevant cues into a workable definition. Selective comparison refers to the process by which new information about a word is related to old information already stored in memory. In addition, the researchers categorize contextual cues into the following: temporal, spatial, value, stative descriptive, functional descriptive, causal/enablement, class membership, and equivalence.

Sternberg (1987) also points out that there are additional factors that determine the success at each of the three stages. One of the factors is how many unknown words are in a text. Obviously, if there are too many unknown words, it is not possible to generate any contextual cues. A lower ratio of unknown to known words provides a better condition for word-meaning inference. There are a few factors that determine contextual helpfulness. For example, it is considered more helpful if the contextual cue is available near the unknown word and if learners possess background knowledge relevant to the situation or topic of the text. In addition, it is considered more helpful if the unknown word appears multiple times in the text and the context for each appearance consistently provides information relevant to the meaning of the unknown word. Furthermore, if the unknown word is crucial for text comprehension, learners are expected to be more likely to engage in word-meaning inference.

2.2.5 Processing Capacity

Daneman (1988) proposed a framework that addresses the processing demand in inferring the meanings of new words during reading. In word-meaning inference, learners are not only expected to obtain information regarding the unknown words, but they also need to integrate various pieces of information in order to decide on what the meanings of the unknown words should be. According to the framework, the integration process involves working memory, which is temporary memory storage (see more in Chapter 4). Working memory enables the learners to maintain the information they are currently processing and connect it to the incoming new information as they read.

Daneman and Green (1986) tested the framework using a reading span test (a working memory measurement). English L1 college students read aloud a set of sentences, and at the end of each set they recalled the last word of each sentence. The students also inferred the meanings of low-frequency words embedded in a text that provided contextual information. The results demonstrated that their reading span scores were related to word-meaning inference success. Similarly, Cain, Oakhill, and Lemmon (2004) found that English L1 children's (nine- and ten-year olds) verbal working memory was related to word-meaning inference ability.

According to this framework, learners who have more cognitive capacity are able to devote more cognitive resources to word-meaning inference. Although the learners' memory capacity is an important factor, how they allocate their cognitive capacity also influences the success of word-meaning inference. It has been suggested that efficient word recognition can free up cognitive capacity for reading comprehension, which requires more elaborate cognitive processing (see more in Chapter 6). Efficient word recognition should also free up capacity for word-meaning inference. Focusing on the role of word recognition, in a college-level ESL study, Hamada and Koda (2010) reported that word recognition efficiency was related to word-meaning inference ability.

2.3 Effectiveness of Incidental Word Learning from Reading

2.3.1 Earlier Studies with Native-Speaking Children

Studies that examined the effectiveness of incidental word learning from reading generally employed a research method that replicated a naturally occurring situation, in which someone unexpectedly learned new words while reading. Because the learning needed to occur incidentally, no special attention was drawn to target words, and no announcement about upcoming tests was given to students beforehand. Learning success was typically measured by the understanding of the meanings of unfamiliar words, which the students were supposed to be able to learn (or infer) from a text they read.

One of the earlier studies is by Nagy, Herman, and Anderson (1985). In the study, eighth graders read a text (approximately 1,000 words containing fifteen target words), and immediately after reading, they completed the following two tasks on the target words: an individual interview that elicited definitions and a multiple-choice definition-matching test. The probability of word-knowledge gain (how many target words' meanings were learned) was about 11 percent in the interview and was about 15 percent in the multiple-choice test.

Similar percentages were reported by Shu, Anderson, and Zhang (1995), who examined the effectiveness of word learning from reading with third and fifth graders in two different L1 groups, English L1 and Chinese L1. After reading two texts, the children completed a multiple-choice definition-matching test. The probability of word learning was about 10 percent for the English L1 children and about 8 percent for the Chinese L1 children. Swanborn and de Glopper (1999) also reported that the average percentage of word leaning from reading was 15 percent, based on a meta-analysis of existing studies.

Although the probability of incidental word learning from reading does not appear to be very high, the studies with native-speaking children uniformly suggest that it is a useful method that all children should take advantage of. The underlying assumption is that even a small percentage of learning success can contribute to the development of word knowledge because school-age children encounter a great deal of words. For example, if they encounter 10,000 unfamiliar words, they could learn 1,000–1,500 of them from reading. The research also agrees that it is essential for children to read extensively, which provides them more opportunities for incidental word learning to occur.

2.3.2 Earlier Studies with L2 Learners

L2 studies generally supported the claim made by the studies with native-speaking children. One of the earlier findings came from the work by Pitts,

White, and Krashen (1989), a replication study of Saragi, Nation, and Meister (1978), in which adult English L1 participants read *A Clockwork Orange* (Burgess, 1972) and learned (inferred) the meanings of nadsat words, slang words of Russian origin. In the Pitts et al. study, the participants were college-level ESL students. They read the first two chapters of the book (approximately 6,700 words), including the thirty target nadsat words. Immediately after reading the chapters, the experimental group completed a multiple-choice definition-matching test on the target words. On the other hand, the control group did not read the text and completed the test. The findings overall indicated that the experimental group scored 7.29 percent, whereas the control group scored near zero.

Subsequent studies reported higher percentages of vocabulary gain. For example, Day, Omura, and Hiramatsu (1991) assigned Japanese EFL high school and college students to either a treatment group who read a text (approximately 1,000 words containing seventeen target words) or a control group who did not read the text. A multiple-choice definition-matching test on the target words demonstrated that the treatment group scored 42.76 percent and the control group scored 30.53 percent, indicating a difference of 12.23 percent.

Dupuy and Krashen (1993) assigned college-level English L1 learners of French to either an experimental group who read the script of the film, *Trois hommes et un couffin* (approximately fifteen pages containing thirty target words) or a control group who neither read the script nor watched the film. A multiple-choice definition-matching test on the target words demonstrated that the experimental group scored 49.1 percent, while the control group scored 26.93 percent, indicating a difference of 22.17 percent.

2.3.3 Incidental Word Learning through Extensive Reading

Studies have also examined the effectiveness of incidental word learning during extensive reading (see Chapter 1). For example, in a study by Horst, Cobb, and Meara (1998), ESL students at a university in Oman read a simplified version of Tomas Hardy's *The Mayor of Casterbridge* written by Jones (1979), which contained approximately 21,000 words, over a ten-day period. Two vocabulary tests were administered on the target words from the book before and after the reading: a multiple-choice definition-matching test and a meaning-association test. For the multiple-choice test, the pretest was 48.09 percent and the posttest was 58.36 percent, indicating a 10.27 percent increase in the posttest. For the meaning-association test, the pretest was 42.54 percent and the posttest was 51.62 percent, indicating a 9.08 percent increase in the posttest. The findings demonstrated that incidental word learning from reading was beneficial for L2 learners.

Findings based on case studies with adult L2 learners provided additional support for the benefit of extensive reading in incidental word learning from reading, as reported by Leung (2002) with a Chinese L1 learner of Japanese, Pigada and Schmitt (2006) with a Greek L1 learner of French, and Senoo and Yonemoto (2014) with a Finnish-French-English L1 learner of Japanese.

Studies have also examined the effects of extensive reading as an instructional method involving larger numbers of students (e.g., Elley and Mangubhai, 1983; Horst, 2005). For example, Horst (2005) administered a six-week extensive reading program to adult ESL students in Montreal, Canada. In the program, the students read graded books independently at home with some activities that supported their extensive reading. The students read on average 10.52 books during the program. The self-assessments administered before and after the program indicated that the students gained 17 percent of the 100 target words tested.

Likewise, Webb, and Chang (2015a) administered an extensive reading program to Taiwanese L1 ESL students (tenth graders) during two academic terms, over thirty-seven weeks. The vocabulary gain from the two terms, measured by a multiple-choice definition-matching test, demonstrated that there was on average 41.16 percent of gain one week after the program and 36.6 percent of gain three months after the program. The results also indicated that the gains were much higher for the students who had higher proficiency and more vocabulary knowledge, suggesting that proficiency level would need to be considered when evaluating the effectiveness of extensive reading programs.

2.3.4 Drawing Attention to Unfamiliar Words

The studies summarized earlier are categorized as incidental learning studies because they avoided drawing students' attention to target words. There is a line of research that uses a method where focused attention is drawn to the target words by underlining or bold facing them. For example, Konopak et al. (1987) asked eleventh graders to read a US history text (approximately 1,500 words), which contained ten target words. An intentional-learning group read the text with the target words underlined, while an incidental learning group read the text without the words underlined. The control group read a different passage that did not include the target words. A definition-writing test administered before and after reading indicated that the intentional group had the largest gain among the groups. The intentional group scored 39.65 percent in the pretest and 72.15 percent in the posttest, indicating a gain of 32.5 percent. The incidental group scored 37.28 percent in the pretest and 54.05 percent in the posttest, indicating a gain of 16.77 percent. The control group scored 35.23 percent in the pretest and 39.55 percent in the posttest, indicating a gain of 4.32 percent.

Nassaji and his colleagues' ESL studies followed a similar method, although they analyzed think-aloud data to assess learning outcome. In an earlier study (Nassaji, 2003a), college-level ESL students read a short text (374 words) and inferred the meanings of ten target words that were underlined. The overall accuracy of meaning inference was 25.6 percent. Likewise, in a subsequent study (Hu and Nassaji, 2012), college-level ESL students read a short text (484 words) and inferred the meanings of ten target words that were underlined. The overall accuracy was 54.6 percent immediately after the reading session and 27.1 percent one week later, indicating a 27.5 percent decline.

In Pulido (2009), English L1 college-level learners of Spanish L2 read a short text (approximately 180 words) and inferred the meanings of eight nonsense words, which were bold faced and underlined. The task required the students to write the definition or L1 translation of each target word. There were two types of texts, one with a topic that was more familiar to the students and one with a topic that was less familiar to them. The accuracy of word-meaning inference was 73.25 percent for the more familiar passage and 40.75 percent for the less familiar passage, indicating an overall 57 percent accuracy. Note that these studies did not involve any additional tasks associated with reading. Therefore, they can be categorized as "incidental" learning studies depending on how "incidental" is defined. The findings altogether seem to imply that simply drawing attention to unfamiliar or target words can improve word learning success.

2.3.5 Retention of Words Learned Incidentally from Reading

Several L2 studies have focused on addressing how well learners retain the words learned from reading. For example, in a study with English L1 college students in second year Spanish courses, Knight (1994) compared the performance between a group who read short texts (each containing approximately 250 words) without using a dictionary (exposure group) and a group who did not read the texts (no-exposure group). One of the outcome measurements was a multiple-choice definition-matching test, administered immediately after and two weeks after reading. The test administered immediately after the learning session indicated that the no-exposure group scored 7.5 percent, while the exposure group scored 36.46 percent, indicating a difference of 28.96 percent. In the delayed test, the exposure group scored 33.58 percent, indicating a 2.88 percent decline in the latter test.

Studies by Pulido and her colleagues were also conducted with English L1 college-level Spanish L2 learners. In an earlier study (Pulido, 2003), the students read four short texts, each of which was approximately 170 words long and contained eight nonsense words that served as the target words whose meanings were to be inferred. The learning outcome was measured by a definition-writing test and a multiple-choice definition-matching test two days and twenty-eight days after reading. Overall means for the definition-writing test were 3.13 percent at two days after and 2.88 percent at twenty-eight days after, indicating a 0.25 percent decline in the latter test. Overall means for the multiple-choice test were 28.25 percent at two days after and 26.88 percent at twenty-eight days after, indicating a 1.37 percent decline in the latter test. In a subsequent study (Pulido and Hambrick, 2008) using a similar method, the overall means from a multiple-choice definition-matching test were 28.44 percent for the immediate test and 26.88 percent for the delayed test, indicating a 1.56 percent decline in the latter test.

Unlike the studies mentioned earlier, Waring and Takaki (2003) reported larger declines in a delayed test. College-level Japanese L1 EFL learners read *A little princess* (approximately 6,000 words), including twenty-five pseudowords that replaced original words. The learning outcome tests included a word-form recognition test, a multiple-choice recognition test, and a definition-writing test, all of which were administered immediately after, one week after, and three months after reading. The scores on the word-form recognition test averaged 61.2 percent immediately after, 44.4 percent at one week after (a 16.8 percent decline), and 33.6 percent at three months after (a 27.6 percent decline from the immediate test). The multiple-choice test scores averaged 42.4 percent immediately after, 31.6 percent at one week after (a 10.8 percent decline), and 24.4 percent at three months after (an 18 percent decline from the immediate test). The definition-writing test scores averaged 18.4 percent immediately after, 7.6 percent at one week after (a 10.8 percent decline), and 3.6 percent at three months after (a 14.8 percent decline from the immediate test). The researchers concluded that word learning from reading may not be as effective as expected in the long term.

2.3.6 Comparison of Meaning-Inferred and Meaning-Given Methods

If students can learn new words incidentally from reading, can the method replace traditional vocabulary instruction that is more intentional? This question was investigated in the research that compared a meaning-inferred method, in which learners inferred the meanings of new words, and a meaning-given method, in which learners memorized definitions that provided the meanings. In a study with adult learners of Dutch L2, Hulstijn (1992) compared the following learning methods in the first experiment: translation (L1 translations of each target word provided in the margin of a text), concise context (a sentence clue for each target word provided in the margin), multiple-choice (four meaning options for each target word provided in the margin), and control (no information in the margin).

After reading the text, the learners completed two unannounced tests: a meaning test (write down the meanings of the target words) and a form test (fill in the target words in the original text). In the meaning test, the translation method scored 25.83 percent, which was significantly higher than the other methods (the concise context 16.67 percent, the multiple choice 16.67 percent, the control 7.5 percent). In the form test, there was no significant difference between the methods, and the overall mean across the conditions was 13.54 percent. These results demonstrated that a method that requires the learners to infer the meanings of unfamiliar words from reading was not the most effective in L2, as reported in L1 research (e.g., Nagy, Anderson, and Herman, 1987).

Similarly, in Mondria (2003), Dutch L1 Grade 11 students learned French words in either the meaning-inferred method or the meaning-given (L1 translation) method. A definition-writing test, which measured their learning outcome, revealed that accuracy was similar between the two methods, demonstrating 47 percent in the meaning-inferred and 50 percent in the meaning-given method. Because the meaning-inferred method was more time-consuming, the researcher concluded that the method would not be as effective as suggested. There are more findings confirming the superiority of the meaning-given method, such as Qian (1996) with college-level Chinese L1 EFL students, Laufer (2006) with Israeli EFL students and Barcroft (2009) with Spanish L2 college students. These studies overall suggest that the meaning-given method (or intentional word learning) using L1 translation or L2 definitions is more effective than incidental learning where the meanings need to be inferred.

2.4 Chapter Summary

This chapter reviewed the mechanism of word learning from reading. The first section described the nature of word knowledge, pointing out that knowing a word is not all or nothing. Word knowledge consists of multiple aspects, including form, meaning, and use, and develops incrementally. The second section of the chapter summarized existing frameworks in word learning from reading. Although each framework offers a unique perspective on the word learning mechanism, they all indicate that word learning from reading involves multilevel processes. Students need to discover unknown aspects of word knowledge (word meanings) by making use of various knowledge sources and skills related to reading. Although word learning from reading may appear to occur naturally through reading, the mechanism that makes the learning possible is quite complex, involving multiple factors. Students' linguistic ability is undoubtedly one of the factors that determine the success of word learning.

The last section in this chapter reviewed the effectiveness of incidental word learning from reading. The effectiveness, based on accuracy and retention of inferred meanings, seems to vary across studies. A comparison between incidental and intentional word learning also indicates that the meaning-inferred method may not be as effective as expected for L2 learners. As L1 research suggests (e.g., Nagy, Anderson, and Herman, 1987), even though the success rate is relatively low, if word learning can occur as a by-product of reading, it is still beneficial for students. However, it needs to be noted that students have to read a large amount of material regularly in order to benefit from word learning from reading. Low-level L2 learners may find it difficult to accomplish the expected amount of reading.

3

Factors in Word Learning from Reading

Students are able to learn new words incidentally from reading, yet we cannot assume that all learning attempts result in success. In the studies introduced in this chapter, word-learning success is typically measured by knowledge of word meaning (ability to define/identify the new words' meanings) and/or word form (ability to spell/identify the new words' forms). This chapter categorizes the factors that influence learning success into three sections. The first section summarizes the linguistic characteristics of words that influence their learnability. The section also describes strategy use, which addresses how effectively students use their linguistic knowledge and metacognitive ability in word learning processes. The second section describes the factors related to contextual helpfulness and the frequency of encounters with new words in a text. These text-inherent factors determine the quality of the texts, which influences word learning success. The last section introduces different conditions in which incidental word learning can be implemented. Students may simply read a text or they may read it and work on reading-related tasks and exercises. The last section also offers insights into the types of instruction that lead to better learning outcomes.

3.1 Linguistic Factors and Strategies

3.1.1 Vocabulary Knowledge and Known Word Coverage

Accurate comprehension of a text is essential in learning words from reading. One of the most important factors in reading comprehension is vocabulary knowledge, which is often measured by the knowledge of word families. Word family refers to a set of morphologically related words, such as *observe*, *observable*, and *observation*. Using word-family count, studies involving college-level ESL learners have investigated the threshold vocabulary knowledge necessary for reading comprehension. For instance, Laufer (1992) suggested that 3,000 word families are the minimum required for comprehension of the texts for standardized tests used in the Netherlands. Similarly, Hirsh and Nation (1992) suggested that about 3,000 word families are necessary for comprehension of graded readers. For unsimplified texts, studies have reported that 5,000 word families are necessary (Hirsh and Nation, 1992; Nation and Wang, 1999).

The threshold vocabulary knowledge for reading comprehension is also estimated by the percentage of known word coverage within a text. Studies seem to agree that at least 98 percent of words should be known to learners for the comprehension of unsimplified texts (e.g., Hirsh and Nation, 1992; Hu and Nation, 2000). In a more recent study by Nation (2006), 98 percent coverage equals the knowledge of approximately 3,000 word families for graded readers and 8,000–9,000 word families for novels and newspapers.

Regarding the threshold vocabulary knowledge for word learning from reading, Liu and Nation (1985) compared the success of word-meaning inference in texts with differing known word coverage (96 percent vs. 90 percent). As predicted, their participants outperformed in the text with a higher percentage of known word coverage. Apparently, learners should not try to infer the meanings of unknown words if they do not know most of the words in the text. They might be able to infer the meanings of the new words based on the word-form (e.g., morphology), but their inferences may not be accurate if the contextual information, based on reading comprehension, is not incorporated in inferencing. Coady (1997) suggests that the 3,000 most frequent words should be explicitly taught, especially to beginning-level learners, before attempting word-meaning inference.

3.1.2 Semantic Factors

Semantic factors refer to the characteristics of the meanings of words to be learned. One such factor is the difference between concrete meanings (e.g., *chair*) and abstract meanings (e.g., *friendship*). Pichette, de Serres, and Lafontaine (2012) hypothesized that concrete words would be easier to learn because they provided learners with clearer mental imagery. In the study, French L1 college-level ESL students inferred the meanings of target words (concrete words and abstract words) embedded in sentences. The learning outcome was measured by an unannounced definition-writing test, in which the students wrote down the target words that matched the L1 definitions. In a test administered immediately after the learning session, the students scored higher for the concrete words than the abstract words. However, the difference disappeared in a delayed test one week after the learning session.

In L2 word learning, the semantic difference between L1 and L2 words is perhaps the most critical factor that needs to be considered. Generally speaking, it is easier to learn an L2 word that has an L1 translation equivalent than an L2 word that does not have an L1 translation equivalent. This is because if the translation equivalent exists, learners do not need to construct a new meaning through L2 reading. Paribakht (2005) examined the effects of L1 lexicalization—whether there are lexical equivalents in L1 (single or compound lexical items, including lexical phrases)—in word-meaning inference during reading with college-level Persian L1 EFL students. Using the think-aloud technique (verbalization of thoughts during inferencing), the students read texts and inferred the meanings of the target words, such as *decay* (lexicalized) and *prognosis* (nonlexicalized). As predicted, they were less successful for the nonlexicalized words. The same results were obtained in subsequent studies, Paribakht and Tréville (2007), with college-level French L1 and Persian L1 ESL students, and Chen and Truscott (2010) with Mandarin L1 college-level ESL students. Moreover, Webb (2007a) reported that words whose synonyms were familiar to learners were easier to learn than words whose synonyms were unfamiliar.

3.1.3 Morphological Factors

Morphological factors address how the structure and complexity of word parts influence word learning from reading. One type of morphologically complex words is derived words. In inferring the meanings of derived words, learners make use of their knowledge of roots and affixes (prefixes and suffixes). For example, the word, *unhappiness,* is made up of *un*, a prefix that indicates the meaning of negation (not) or opposite, the root, *happy*, and *-ness*, a suffix that creates a noun from an adjective and indicates a state or quality. Making use of roots and affixes in word-meaning inference is considered to be a beneficial strategy. For example, McCutchen and Logan (2011) asked English L1 Grades

5 and 8 students to infer the meanings of unfamiliar words that were shown in sentences. The researchers found that the students were more accurate in inferring the meanings of the words with a familiar word part (e.g., *verbose*) than the words without a familiar word part (e.g., *prolix*). L2 studies have also reported that L2 learners commonly made use of word parts, including both derivational (e.g., *happy—happi<u>ness</u>*) and inflectional morphemes (e.g., past tense *-ed*, plural *-s*) in inferring the meanings of unfamiliar words (e.g., Chern, 1993; Paribakht and Wesche, 1999).

Another type of morphologically complex words is compound words, which are made up of multiple roots. According to Selkirk (1982), English compound words are categorized into the following types: noun + noun (e.g., *spaceship*), verb + noun (e.g., *playground)*, noun + verb (e.g., *browbeat*), adjective + verb (e.g., *dry clean*), and verb + particle (e.g., *pick up*). In inferring the meanings of compound words, learners make use of the known roots. For instance, Chern (1993) reported that Chinese EFL students were able to infer the meaning of *woodpecker* by making use of the familiar root word, *wood*.

Although making use of known word parts is useful, it should be noted that some word parts provide misleading information about the meanings of the words, because they are semantically opaque, that is, unrelated or remotely related to the meanings of the words. For instance, Nagy (1997) points out that the meaning of *casualty* is not inferable from *casual*. For compound words with two roots, four semantic types are possible, where T denotes transparent and O denotes opaque (Libben, 1998; Libben et al., 2003): TT (e.g., *carwash*), OT (e.g., *strawberry*), TO (e.g., *jailbird*), and OO (e.g., *hogwash*).

More recently, Hamada (2014) examined the role of semantic opaqueness in word-meaning inference using sentences that included pseudo-compounds (e.g., *sadmesk*). There were two sentence conditions, transparent and opaque. In the transparent condition, both the known constituent of the pseudoword (*sad*) and the sentence context provided a clue relevant to the meaning of the pseudo-compound, whereas in the opaque condition, the known constituent provided a misleading clue that did not match the sentence context. The results from college-level ESL students indicated that the students at a lower proficiency level chose meanings based solely on the known constituents even though the meanings did not match the context. A similar conclusion was reported by Mori and Nagy (1999) in a study with college-level learners of Japanese L2.

3.1.4 Orthographic Factors

The word, *orthography*, is derived from two Greek roots, orthos (*correct*) and graphein (*to write*). Orthographic knowledge refers to the knowledge about how a word should be written or spelled. For example, we need to be able to tell the difference between *meat* and *meet* in order to differentiate their meanings. We also need to be able to spell words following the orthographic rules for the language. In English, the letter sequence *cl* is common in the word initial position (e.g., clean, cliff), while the letter sequence *ckl* is not permitted in the word initial position.

One might predict that orthographically less-common words are more difficult to learn. Bordag et al. (2017) examined how orthographic probability (sequential letter probability) influences word learning from reading in German. In the incidental learning experiment, a native-speaking group and an L2 group learned pseudowords with high orthographic probability (e.g., *Pend*) and pseudowords with low orthographic probability (e.g., *Wrix*). Against the expectation, the native-speaking group learned more successfully in the low probability condition, which was attributed to the fact that the rareness of the spelling drew more attention from the students. Unlike the native-speaking group, the L2 group did not demonstrate any differences between the high and low probability conditions.

Cognate status is another factor related to orthographic characteristics. Cognates are words that share similar spelling and meanings between multiple languages, due to the fact that they come from the same source (McCarthy, 1990). In English, there are many words borrowed from Latin and French, some of which are cognates in multiple languages, such as the following: intelligent (English), intelligent (French), inteligente (Spanish), intelligente (Italian), and inteligente (Portuguese). Findings suggest that L2 learners make use of their knowledge of cognates in word learning. For example, Paribakht and Wesche (1999) found that college-level ESL students made use of French cognates, such as *suffisant* and *controversé*, in word-meaning inference. Nevertheless, false cognates, words whose spellings are similar but are unrelated in meaning, can cause difficulty (e.g., Bensoussan and Laufer, 1984).

3.1.5 Knowledge Sources and Strategy Use

Learners use various knowledge sources and strategies when they infer the meanings of unknown words encountered during reading. Studies conducted on this topic typically use the think-aloud technique to capture the learners' thought processes. For example, De Bot, Paribakht, and Wesche (1997) reported that college-level ESL students used knowledge of sentence-level grammar, word morphology, and world (e.g., topic of the text) for inferring the meanings of unknown words.

Subsequent studies compiled more detailed lists of knowledge sources and strategies. In a study with college-level EFL students, Nassaji (2003a) categorized the knowledge sources the students used into five types: grammatical, morphological, world, L1 (translating a word into L1), and discourse (relations between or within sentences and devices that connect different parts of the text). The strategies they used were categorized into six types: repeating, verifying, self-inquiry, analyzing, monitoring, and word-form analogy. The think-aloud data indicated that the students preferred to use world knowledge (46.2 percent) most frequently, followed by morphological knowledge (26.9 percent) and grammatical knowledge (11.5 percent). As for strategy use, they preferred to use word repeating (39.7 percent) most frequently, followed by section repeating (24.0 percent) and analogy (8.5 percent).

The knowledge sources and strategies that led to a better rate of inference success turned out to be slightly different from what the students preferred to use. As for the knowledge sources, morphological knowledge (0.93) had the highest success, followed by world knowledge (0.83) and discourse knowledge (0.78). As for the strategies, verifying (1.51) had the highest success, followed by self-inquiry (1.15) and section repeating (1.05). These findings suggest that the students used a variety of knowledge sources and strategies, but not every source or strategy led to success in word-meaning inference.

In a study with Chinese L1 college-level ESL students, Hu and Nassaji (2014) categorized the strategies into three types: form-focused (making use of information from an unknown word), meaning-focused (making use of contextual information), and evaluation (metacognitive strategies to oversee inferencing performance). The results indicated that the successful students were aware of the gap in their knowledge and made use of the meaning-focused strategies more frequently. In contrast, the less successful students used the strategies in a random and unrelated manner and tended to rely more on the form-focused strategies.

Wesche and Paribakht (2010) is one of the few studies that examined cross-linguistic influence on word-meaning inference. By comparing three groups of readers with typologically different linguistic backgrounds (English, Persian, and French), the researchers aimed to find out whether there would be L1 transfer in the type of knowledge sources preferred by L2 learners during word-meaning inference. In the study, all participant groups performed the task in L1, and the Persian and French groups also performed the task in their L2 English, which was compared to their L1 inferencing behaviors. The major difference between the L2 groups was that the Persian group depended more on discourse cues, whereas the French participants depended more on word-related cues, such as word morphology, word form, and word association. These differences were found both in their L1 and L2 word-meaning inference, suggesting that L1 word-meaning inference processes transfer to L2 word-meaning inference.

The studies introduced earlier mainly reported the kinds of knowledge sources and strategies learners tended to use. Kern (1989) approached strategy use from an instructional standpoint. In the study, college-level English L1 learners of French received strategy instruction for an eight-week period through both in-class work and homework. The instruction included the teaching of strategies, such as morphological and orthographic analysis, sentence analysis (making use of cohesive and logical relationships), discourse analysis, and reading for specific purposes (skimming and scanning for specific details). The results demonstrated that the strategy instruction significantly improved the students' reading comprehension but did not show any reliable effects on the success of word-meaning inference during reading.

3.2 Contextual Helpfulness and Frequency of Encounters

3.2.1 Contextual Helpfulness

In an effort to categorize kinds of contextual information learners use for word learning from reading, Chern (1993) used the terms, local cues and global cues, based on where in the text the contextual information was generated from. Local cues referred to the contextual information generated from the sentence where the target word was embedded. Global cues referred to the contextual information generated in the sentences before and after the target word, which required the students to read and comprehend a larger portion of the text. The results based on the think-aloud data from college-level Chinese ESL students demonstrated that global cues were used more frequently by the students with more advanced proficiency.

The quality of contextual information influences the success of word learning from reading. For example, Beck, McKeown, and McCaslin (1983) found that the contextual information available in children's stories varied in degree of directness: misdirective (directs students to an incorrect meaning), nondirective (does not direct students to any meaning), general (directs students to a general meaning), and directive (directs students to a correct meaning). In order to test whether these differences in context would influence the success of word learning, the researchers asked adult English L1 participants to read the stories and infer the meanings of target words that were left blank. The accuracy of meaning inference varied according to the directness of the context: 86 percent in the directive, 49 percent in the general, 27 percent in the nondirective, and 3 percent in the misdirective. The findings demonstrated that not all texts were written in a way that provided relevant contextual information for word-meaning inference.

L2 studies also have suggested that contextual informativeness influences the success of word-meaning inference. For example, in a study with Spanish L2 college students, Frantzen (2003) found that inaccurate inference was largely due to the vagueness or ambiguity of contextual information. Furthermore, Pulido (2007) demonstrated that students were more successful in word-meaning inference when reading a text on a familiar topic. Presumably, they were able to comprehend the text on the familiar topic better, which helped them generate contextual information more effectively.

Nevertheless, Zahar, Cobb, and Spada (2001) reported that contextual informativeness was not related to word gain among Grade 7 ESL students in Quebec. In addition, there are studies suggesting that learners' proficiency level, including overall L2 skill, reading comprehension skill, and vocabulary knowledge, relates to how well they are able to make use of contextual information (Horst, Cobb, and Meara, 1998; Jenkins, Stein, and Wysocki, 1984; Kondo-Brown, 2006; Mulder et al., 2019; Pulido, 2007). Although the contextual informativeness of the text is certainly important, it seems clear that contextual informativeness is not the only factor that determines word learning success.

3.2.2 Frequency of Encounters

Frequency of encounters refers to how many times the target words appear in a text. Because more frequent encounters are considered to provide more contextual information, it is commonly assumed that more encounters lead to better word learning (e.g., Godfroid et al., 2018; Jenkins, Stein, and Wysocki, 1984). How many encounters are necessary? For instance, in a study by Rott (1999), English L1 college students who were enrolled in a fourth semester German class inferred the meanings of target words embedded in texts, which varied in the number of times the target words appeared (two, four, or six times). The learning outcomes, measured by a definition-writing and a multiple-choice definition-matching task, demonstrated that two and four encounters resulted in similar word knowledge gain, whereas six encounters resulted in significantly more gain. Similarly, in a study with college-level ESL students, Horst, Cobb, and Meara (1998) suggested that sizable learning gains were more likely to occur if target words appeared eight times or more in a passage.

Recently, more findings are pointing to the effects of frequency of encounters on different aspects of word knowledge. For example, Pellicer-Sánchez and Schmitt (2010) found that after ten encounters, Spanish L1 college-level ESL students' scores on recognition tests differed between word meaning (84 percent) and word-form (76 percent). On the other hand, Mohamed (2018), measuring ESL college students' eye movement during reading, reported that multiple encounters increased word-form recognition, but did not improve meaning recall nor meaning recognition. As Webb (2007b) suggested, more than ten encounters would probably be necessary to develop more comprehensive knowledge of a word.

Nonetheless, some studies found no correlations between frequency of encounters and word learning (e.g., Webb and Chang, 2015b). Interestingly, Kweon and Kim (2008) found that Korean L1 college-level EFL students learned words with a lower frequency of encounters better than words with a higher frequency of encounters, when the less frequently encountered words were crucial to reading comprehension. Moreover, Pagán and Nation (2019) reported that English L1 college students learned more words when they encountered unfamiliar words multiple times in different contexts, rather than in the same context. These findings imply that the quality of contextual information for each encounter needs to be taken into consideration when discussing the role of contextual information in word learning from reading.

3.3 Reading-Related Tasks and Instruction

3.3.1 Tasks That Accompany Reading

Some studies maintain that reading alone does not provide sufficient input for word learning to occur (see Chapter 2). It has been shown that word learning is more effective if reading is accompanied by tasks, in specific, output-production tasks, which provide learners with an opportunity to use the target words (e.g., Eckerth and Tavakoli, 2012; Joe, 1995, 1998; de Leeuw, Segers, and Verhoeven, 2014; Sun, 2017). Meta-analyses that reviewed L1 and L2 studies also suggest that output tasks increase word learning success (Huang, Eslami, and Wilson, 2012; Kuhn and Stahl, 1998).

There are a number of findings that have reported on the benefits of output tasks. For instance, Joe (1995, 1998) reported that reading and retelling enhanced word learning, suggesting that these tasks facilitated a higher level of generation, which involved more elaboration on the words' specific properties and associations. De Leeuw, Segers, and Verhoeven (2014) compared the effectiveness of a reading-only task and a reading-plus task in an L1 study with Dutch-speaking fifth graders. In the reading-plus task, one of the following tasks accompanied reading: filling in blanks in the text with words, answering text-comprehension questions, or writing a summary. The question-answering and summary-writing tasks were more effective than the reading-only or the blank-filling tasks.

More recently, Sun (2017) examined the effects of a collaborative output activity on word learning from reading. Taiwanese L1 EFL college students received instruction on one of the following methods: reading only, reading plus explicit explanation of inferencing strategies, or reading plus a group activity that involved discussion of the text. The researcher found that reading plus explicit explanation of inferencing strategies was most effective for short-term word learning, but reading plus a group activity was the most effective for long-term word learning.

3.3.2 Glosses and Dictionaries

A number of L2 studies investigated the effectiveness of the use of glosses (L1 translations or definitions of target words) and a dictionary in word learning from reading (e.g., Hulstijn, Hollander, and Greidanus, 1996; Peters et al., 2009; Rott, 2005, 2007; Rott and Williams, 2003). For instance, Peters et al. (2009) reported that looking up the meanings of unknown words in a dictionary and writing L2 synonyms/definitions or an L1 translation of the words increased word learning success more than reading only. Moreover, Rott (2005) found that multiple-choice glosses, in which English L1 college students of German L2 were given four options of L1 translations for each target word, were more effective than typical single-word glosses, in which the students were given the L1 translation for each target word. The superiority of the multiple-choice glosses was attributed to the fact that the choices induced more elaborative processing of the target words. Nevertheless, Watanabe (1997) did not find any differences between the single and multiple-choice glosses in a study with Japanese L1 college-level EFL students.

Furthermore, Barcroft (2015) focused on the processes involved in retrieving target words' information and examined different conditions related to glosses. College-level Spanish L1 EFL students read a text, in which target words appeared three times. In a read-only condition, the text included the target words and their L1 translations all three times. In contrast, in a read-retrieval-production condition, the target words and their L1 translations appeared only the first time. For the second and third times, the students were given only the L1 translations and were asked to write down the matching target words on their own. The researcher found that the read-retrieval-production task was significantly more effective for word learning than the read-only task.

In addition, findings from computer-assisted language learning studies have reported the effects of glosses in learning words from multimedia reading materials. For instance, Yoshii and Flaitz (2002) compared three different glosses, text (definition)-only, picture-only, and text and picture, in a study with Japanese L1 college-level EFL students. They found that the gloss with both text and picture resulted in better word learning outcome than the glosses with only one type of information. Examining the presentation of glosses, Türk and Erçetin (2014) compared the effectiveness of a simultaneous display condition, where text (a definition) and a visual image (an image that illustrated the definition) were shown together as a single gloss on the same screen, and an interactive display condition, where the text and visual image were presented on different screens and the students were asked to choose one or the other. The data from Turkish L1 high school students indicated that simultaneous display was more effective for word learning.

3.3.3 Form-Focused and Meaning-Focused Tasks

As introduced in Chapter 1, Laufer (2005, 2010) maintains that focus on form (FonF) and focus on forms (FonFs) instruction, originally proposed for teaching grammar (e.g., Doughty, 2003; Long, 1991), can be applied to the context of word learning from reading. In FonF, reading instruction is accompanied by communicative tasks using authentic materials with more focus on meanings. In contrast, in FonFs, reading instruction is accompanied by tasks that focus on target words, including structural aspects of the words. Both types of instruction contribute to word learning more effectively than reading only, but most findings seem to suggest that FonFs is more effective than FonF (e.g., Hill and Laufer, 2003; Laufer and Rozovski-Roitblat, 2011, 2015; Peters, 2012).

For instance, Laufer and Rozovski-Roitblat (2015) compared the effectiveness of the following three tasks on word learning: reading only, reading with FonF, and reading with FonFs. In reading with FonF, in addition to reading, college-level EFL students looked up the meanings of unfamiliar words in a dictionary and also answered multiple-choice comprehension questions. In reading with FonFs, in addition to reading, the students worked on exercises such as filling in blanks in sentences, matching the target words with their definitions or synonyms, and writing L1 and L2 translations. The results demonstrated that reading with FonFs was the most effective of the three task types.

Drawing from the lexical quality hypothesis (Perfetti and Hart, 2002) (see more in Chapter 4), Elgort et al. (2018) compared the effectiveness of a form-focused elaboration (writing down the target words) and a meaning-focused elaboration (writing down the inferred meanings of the words). In the study, Chinese L1 and Dutch L1 college students learned English words shown in sentence contexts in one of the elaboration tasks, followed by a meaning-verification presentation, in which the students were shown the definitions of the words. The results indicated that the form-focused elaboration was more effective for word learning than the meaning-focused elaboration. The researchers explained that word writing enabled more precise encoding of a word's form in addition to learning the word's meaning.

3.3.4 Audio-Assisted Reading and Repeated Reading

Do students learn words better through reading or listening? To answer this question, Brown, Waring, and Donkaewbua (2008) compared the effects of three tasks on word learning: reading only, reading while listening, and listening only. The results from college-level Japanese L1 EFL students indicated that they were more successful in the first two tasks, reading while listening (15.68 percent) and reading only (14.64 percent), than listening only (2 percent). Nevertheless, Geva et al. (2017) reported that Hebrew L1 fourth graders were more successful in learning words from listening than reading. The researchers explained that the listening condition helped the children focus more on comprehension because they didn't need to pay attention to decoding words and sentences from the text.

Repeated reading is a task that requires students to read the same text multiple times. Applying the logic from extensive reading research, repeated reading is also expected to contribute to reading comprehension, reading fluency, and word learning from reading (see Taguchi, Takayasu-Maass, and Gorsuch, 2004). Assisted-repeated reading is a variation of repeated reading, in which students listen to reading aloud of a text as they read it. They are typically provided with an audio recording of the text while reading it.

Most findings demonstrate the advantage of assisted-repeated reading. For example, Webb and Chang (2012) instructed middle-school students in Taiwan to read two stories per week at least twice over a fourteen-week period. The unassisted-repeated reading group was provided with only the stories, while the assisted-repeated reading group was provided with the stories along with an audio recording of them. The results indicated that the assisted-repeated reading group learned more words than their counterparts. Similar findings were reported by Han and Chen (2010), in a case study with a heritage learner of Chinese, suggesting that assisted-repeated reading could be a useful pedagogical tool for teaching vocabulary.

3.4 Chapter Summary

This chapter has shown that various factors influence the success of word learning from reading. The linguistic factors introduced are vocabulary knowledge as well as the semantic, morphological, and orthographic characteristic of the words to be learned. Although some words may be inherently more difficult than others due to these characteristics, students' linguistic ability influences the success of word learning from reading. Students also need to make strategic use of their linguistic knowledge while applying metacognitive strategies, such as monitoring, evaluating, and planning. As for the factors coming from texts themselves, encountering the target words repeatedly in rich contexts increases the success of word learning. Nevertheless, it needs to be noted that not all texts are written in a way that provides sufficient contextual information for word learning.

This chapter also reviewed various instructional tasks that have been examined for word learning from reading. While reading leads to more opportunities for word learning than not reading, the most effective approach seems to be reading plus an output-production task. Students need to be engaged in a task that requires them to use the target words, in addition to reading. As a conclusion, it is important to keep in mind that there is no single factor that determines the success of word learning from reading. Multiple factors, some inherent in words/texts and others coming from students' ability, jointly determine word learning success.

Part II

How Do We Obtain Information from Reading and Use It for Word-Meaning Inference?

4

Introducing the Cognitive Model of Word-Meaning Inference

This chapter proposes the Cognitive Model of Word-Meaning Inference, which illustrates the connection between the processes involved in reading and the processes involved in word-meaning inference. Before introducing the model, it is important to understand the mechanisms of reading processes. The first section of the chapter introduces the models based on L1 reading, and the second section introduces theories specific to L2 reading. The third section of the chapter describes the processes learners go through, including how they identify an unknown word and infer its meaning, referring to an example passage. The last section of the chapter details how the Cognitive Model of Word-Meaning Inference works, focusing on how learners obtain the two types of critical information, word-form and contextual information, and make use of them for word-meaning inference.

4.1 Cognitive Models of Reading Processes

4.1.1 Component Skills Approach

The component skills approach, proposed by Carr and Levy (1990: 5), assumes that reading is a "product of a complex but decomposable information-processing system." Under this approach, reading processes can be separated into underlying processes that are interrelated with one another. The component skills approach aims to identify the components of reading, as well as the degree of contribution of each component to reading comprehension and to the other components. The findings often have direct pedagogical implications, indicating which components contribute to the development of reading ability.

Among different components, research has suggested that phonological awareness plays a critical role in reading development (e.g., Goswami and Bryant, 1990a; Liberman and Shankweiler, 1991; Wagner and Torgesen, 1987). Phonological awareness is awareness of the sound system of a language (e.g., the ability to identify how many phonemes are in a word). A majority of the findings that demonstrated the critical role of phonological awareness come from English-speaking children (e.g., Mann, 1991), yet there are some findings from children whose native languages are other than English, such as Arabic (Tibi and Kirby, 2018) and German (Wimmer et al., 1991).

The contribution of phonological awareness has also been investigated together with morphological awareness, which is awareness of the word-internal structure and its corresponding meaning. For example, in a longitudinal study with English L1 children from Grades 2 to 5, Deacon and Kirby (2004) found that both phonological and morphological awareness significantly contributed to reading comprehension. L2 studies also suggested that morphological awareness contributed to reading comprehension (e.g., Jeon, 2011; Kieffer, Biancarosa, and Mancilla-Martinez, 2013).

Phonological awareness/skill is also important for L2 reading development, but other skills, such as vocabulary knowledge, have been shown to be crucial as well. For example, in a study with advanced-level ESL students (graduate students), Nassaji (2003b) found that word recognition and vocabulary knowledge (lexical-semantic knowledge) were highly correlated with reading comprehension compared to the other skills/knowledge examined (phonological awareness, orthographic awareness, and syntactic knowledge). Nevertheless, a meta-analysis by Jeon and Yamashita (2014) reported slightly different conclusions, suggesting that L2 grammar knowledge, L2 vocabulary knowledge, and L2 phonological decoding were the strongest correlates of L2 reading comprehension.

4.1.2 Information-Processing Approach, Working Memory, and Automaticity

The information-processing approach views reading as the result of extracting and integrating multiple levels of linguistic information from a text. The levels of processing are categorized as either lower level or higher level (Grabe, 2009). Lower-level processing typically includes the processes that enable word recognition (accessing lexical information), which are orthographic, phonological, semantic, and morphological processing. Higher-level processing typically includes syntactic and discourse processing, which are the processes that integrate the information from the lower-level processing for text comprehension.

The information-processing approach also explains the mechanism of reading processes in terms of a cognitive capacity limitation, measured by working memory capacity. Working memory consists of a central module (central executive) and two subcomponents (the phonological loop and the visuo-spatial sketch pad). It has been suggested that the phonological loop, which is a speech-based system, plays a critical role in executing cognitive tasks, including reading and word learning (Baddeley, 1986). Findings demonstrated that readers with a smaller working memory capacity struggle in reading comprehension, due to inefficiency in processing and storing the information extracted during reading (e.g., Baddeley, Logie, and Nimmo-Smith, 1985; Cain, Oakhill, and Bryant, 2004; Daneman and Carpenter, 1983). A similar conclusion was reported by studies with L2 readers (e.g., Erçetin and Alptekin, 2013; Joh and Plakans, 2017; Walter, 2004). Furthermore, Hamada and Koda (2010) demonstrated that word recognition efficiency was critical in L2 word-meaning inference from reading.

In addition, the information-processing approach points out the importance of automaticity in reading processes. Human cognition has a limited capacity and cannot simultaneously handle all levels of processing (LaBerge and Samuels, 1974). Therefore, in order to accomplish multiple levels of processing, some processing must become automatized (Daneman, 1991; Daneman and Carpenter, 1983). That is, some processing needs to be achieved fast, accurately, and effortlessly, without consuming much of the cognitive capacity. Automaticity is not easily accomplished in the higher-level processes because they require unique, rather than routine, operations in each processing instance. In contrast, word recognition (or lower-level processing) can become automatized more easily, because it is a more rule-governed process (see more in Chapter 5). Thus, there is a consensus in reading research that automatized word recognition is crucial for successful reading comprehension (e.g., Adams, 1994; Perfetti, 1985).

4.1.3 Simple View of Reading

The simple view of reading argues that word decoding and listening comprehension skills are the skills primarily responsible for reading comprehension success (Gough, 1996; Gough and Tunmer, 1986; Hoover and Gough, 1990). Decoding refers to the extraction of phonological information, which is the process of converting written scripts/letters into their corresponding sounds. Decoding ability is often measured by an ability to read pseudowords, which are non-existing words that follow the orthographic structure of a language (see more in Chapter 7). According to the simple view of reading, reading comprehension can be described by the following formula, where reading (R) equals the product of decoding (D) and listening comprehension (C).

$$R = D \times C$$

The theory is based on the premise that decoding is a skill specific to written language, and comprehension skills gained from listening comprehension can be applied to reading comprehension. Studies involving native-speaking children provided support for the theory. For example, Tilstra et al. (2009) examined English L1 children at Grades 4, 7, and 9 on various skills, including reading comprehension, word decoding, listening comprehension, vocabulary knowledge, and oral reading fluency. The results demonstrated that the contribution of decoding and listening comprehension to reading comprehension was significant for all grade levels. Interestingly, the contribution differed between the grades, 61 percent for the fourth graders, 48 percent for the seventh graders, and 38 percent for the ninth graders, suggesting that decoding and listening comprehension were more crucial for younger learners who were still developing reading skills. In addition, the results demonstrated that the contribution of decoding was the highest for the fourth graders, and the contribution of listening comprehension increased from the fourth to seventh graders but did not change from the seventh to ninth graders.

The simple view of reading has also been investigated in studies involving primary and secondary school children in various L2s, such as Chinese L2 (Wong, 2017), Dutch L2 (Verhoeven and van Leeuwe, 2012), English L2 (Proctor et al., 2005), and Spanish L2 (Sparks, 2015). Overall, the L2 findings were analogous to those from native-speaking children, indicating the critical contribution of decoding and listening comprehension to reading comprehension. Some studies further pointed out a developmental change, suggesting that the contribution of decoding was larger for lower graders, while the contribution of listening comprehension was larger for middle to upper graders at elementary school (Proctor et al., 2005; Verhoeven and van Leeuwe, 2012).

4.1.4 Interactive Compensatory Model

The interactive compensatory model (Stanovitch, 1984; Stanovich, West, and Feeman, 1981) contends that reading comprehension involves an interactive activation of two processes. One of the processes is to activate semantic memory via word recognition processes, which is expected to occur automatically, consuming a limited amount of cognitive capacity. The other process is a prediction that readers make for a given context. This process operates more slowly, consuming more cognitive capacity because it is specific to each individual context they encounter. The model predicts that when readers struggle in the first process, they end up relying more on the other process in order to comprehend a text.

The empirical findings for the model come from studies that compared word recognition ability between fluent and less fluent readers. For example, Kim and Goetz (1994) tested English L1 third graders with differing reading abilities (high and low) on oral reading of a text which contained altered words created by grapheme substitution, such as, in a sentence about beautiful spring weather, the word *leather* was used instead of *weather*. If the children were able to read the altered word accurately, they were considered to possess high ability in word recognition without being affected by the contextual information. On the other hand, if they read aloud the original word, it was considered that their word recognition was affected by the contextual information. The researchers found that the children with high reading ability were more accurate in reading the altered words.

Moreover, some studies indicated that there was a developmental change in the weight between word recognition and contextual information in reading comprehension. For instance, Goldsmith-Phillips (1989) asked English L1 Grades 2, 4, and 6 children to read passages and analyzed their reading errors qualitatively. The findings suggested that the second graders relied more on contextual information to recognize words, while the sixth graders used their word decoding skill to recognize words. The fourth graders appeared to be in a transitional stage between the reading styles exhibited by the second and sixth graders.

4.1.5 Lexical Quality Hypothesis

The lexical quality hypothesis (Perfetti, 2007; Perfetti and Hart, 2002) claims that the quality of lexical representations that readers possess in their mental lexicons is the most critical factor in reading. The lexical representations include orthography, phonology, grammar, meaning, and constituent binding (a connection between the properties). For example, knowing the most appropriate meaning of the word, *bank*, in the following two sentences, "I am a loan officer at a bank" and "I walked my dog along the bank," requires readers to have higher quality semantic information of the word. Another example is the difference between *slow* and *low*, which requires them to be able to identify the orthographic difference between the two words. Readers who possess higher quality lexical representations are able to retrieve the representations accurately and process them synchronously. As a result, they are able to integrate meanings from a text more efficiently for reading comprehension.

The lexical quality hypothesis is an updated version of the verbal efficiency theory (Perfetti, 1985). Although both theories claim the critical role of word recognition in reading comprehension, the verbal efficiency theory emphasized the processing aspect (word recognition efficiency). It was considered that accurate and automatized word recognition was primarily responsible for reading comprehension success. On the other hand, the lexical quality hypothesis highlights the importance of knowledge of the words to be recognized, including both the size (how many) and depth (how well) of the lexical knowledge.

Some of the empirical tests of the hypothesis come from longitudinal studies (Hersch and Andrews, 2012; Verhoeven and van Leeuwe, 2008; Verhoeven, van Leeuwe, and Vermeer, 2011). For example, in a study with Dutch L1 children from Grades 1 to 6, Verhoeven, van Leeuwe, and Vermeer. (2011) found a reciprocal relationship between their advanced vocabulary and reading comprehension scores, suggesting that the knowledge of word forms and meanings contributes to the development of reading comprehension ability.

4.2 Theories in L2 Reading

4.2.1 L2 Proficiency as a Critical Factor

The models of reading processes introduced in the previous section provide a foundation for understanding the mechanisms of reading, primarily based on research involving participants reading in their L1s. However, there are some factors unique to L2 reading that are not included in the models introduced earlier. In order to illustrate the difference between L1 and L2 reading, this section summarizes theories that explain factors in L2 reading.

Earlier theories in L2 reading comprehension focused on the role of L2 competence, in particular, vocabulary and grammar competencies. Clarke (1980) proposed the short circuit hypothesis, claiming that L2 proficiency was the most important factor in successful L2 reading comprehension. In the study, Spanish L1 ESL learners with different L1 reading abilities (high and low) read aloud texts in Spanish and English. Based on a miscue analysis (analysis of their reading errors), it was concluded that even those who were categorized as high L1 reading ability were not able to use the strategies they used in L1 when they were reading in L2. It was argued that limited control over L2 linguistic ability "short circuited" the good readers' systems in L2.

A similar claim has been made by other researchers, such as Yorio (1971) and Cziko (1980), further suggesting that learners with low L2 proficiency are less successful in reading comprehension because they struggle with lower-level skills before reaching a global understanding of the text. Their studies are within the framework of the linguistic threshold hypothesis, which assumes that a certain level of L2 linguistic competency must first be achieved in order to read in an L2 (see Bernhardt and Kamil, 1995). Moreover, Alderson (1984, 2000) clarifies the role of L2 proficiency in terms of proficiency levels. L2 proficiency is considered to be more critical for lower-proficiency learners, whereas both L2 proficiency and reading-specific skills are considered to be important for more advanced learners. The existing findings seem to agree with this claim, demonstrating that both reading-specific skills (often measured by

L1 reading ability) and L2 proficiency play an important role in L2 reading comprehension (e.g., Schoonen, Hulstijn, and Bossers, 1998; Yamashita, 2002).

4.2.2 L1 Reading Ability as a Critical Factor

The developmental interdependence hypothesis (Cummins, 1979, 1991, 2000) contends that L1 reading ability contributes to L2 reading comprehension, based on the notion of common underlying proficiency. According to the hypothesis, the cognitive processes necessary for performing academic work, including reading, are the same whether it is done in L1 or L2. Therefore, it is considered that once learners acquire competency in L1 reading, they can transfer the skills and strategies they use for L1 reading to L2 reading. The hypothesis has also provided a theoretical basis for the concepts, cognitive academic language proficiency (CALP) and basic interpersonal communication skills (BICS), which are widely accepted in instructional settings.

Much of the empirical support for the hypothesis comes from studies involving L2 readers and bilingual children in primary and secondary schools. For example, in a study with Turkish L1 learners of Dutch L2, Verhoeven (1994) found that their phonological, pragmatic, and reading comprehension skills transferred between the two languages. Sparks et al. (2012) also reported a relationship between L1 reading skills and L2 literacy and oral skills, further suggesting the importance of building L1 literacy skills through a print-rich environment.

4.2.3 Cross-Linguistic Approach

The approach proposed by Koda (2005, 2007) views reading processes from a cross-linguistic perspective, applying the concept of cross-linguistic transfer (Gass and Selinker, 1983; Kellerman and Sharwood Smith, 1986) to reading. The way in which readers process texts written in L2 is influenced by the linguistic characteristics of their L1 and L2. As readers gain more experience reading in L2, the extent of L2 and L1 influence changes, although dual-language involvement is always present in L2 reading.

Koda (2007) explains that L2 reading necessitates three components: decoding, text-information building, and reader-model construction. In decoding, readers extract linguistic information from words. In order to accomplish decoding, they need to possess orthographic knowledge, phonological knowledge, vocabulary (semantic) knowledge, and morphological knowledge. In text-information building, readers integrate the information extracted through decoding into phrases, sentences, and paragraphs. In order to accomplish text-information building, they need to possess syntactic knowledge, discourse knowledge (including the knowledge of discourse markers), and text-structure knowledge. In reader-model construction, readers synthesize the integrated text information with prior knowledge for comprehension. The processing in each of the three components is subject to dual-language influence.

The cross-linguistic approach offers a more detailed account of L1 transfer phenomena, taking into consideration linguistic distance between L1 and L2. For instance, Pasquarella et al. (2015), a study with Spanish-English and Chinese-English bilinguals, found that word reading accuracy transferred between Spanish and English, but not between Chinese and English. However, word reading fluency transferred in both language pairs, suggesting that fluency might be a script-universal skill. Regarding phonological and morphological awareness, some studies found L1-L2 transfer of phonological awareness (e.g., Cisero and Royer, 1995; Durgunoğlu, Nagy, and Hancin-Bhatt, 1993) and morphological awareness (Hayashi and Murphy, 2013; Pasquarella et al., 2011). On the other hand, in a study with Arabic-English bilinguals, Saiegh-Haddad and Geva (2008) reported that phonological awareness was transferred between the two languages, but morphological awareness was not.

Within the cross-linguistic approach, studies have also shown that the linguistic distance between L1 and L2 affects L2 word recognition (e.g., Akamatsu 2003; Hamada and Koda, 2008; Muljani, Koda, and Moates, 1998). For instance, Akamatsu (2003) examined how L1-L2 orthographic distance affects L2 reading comprehension, using passages written with uppercase and lowercase combined letters, such as the following:

HoW dO yOu FeEl wHeN yoU rEaD sEnTEnCeS wRitTeN WiTh uPPer ANd lOwEr CaSe lEtTerS MiXeD uP?

The participants were three groups of college-level ESL students with contrasting L1 orthographic backgrounds: Chinese, Japanese, and Persian. Persian was considered to be closer to the English orthographic system (an alphabetic orthography), while Chinese and Japanese were considered to be more distant from English. The results indicated that the Chinese and Japanese L1 participants were slower in reading the passages than the Persian counterparts, suggesting that L1 orthographic distance affected their reading speed.

4.3 How Do We Infer the Meanings of New Words?

4.3.1 Identifying Known and Unknown Words

This section illustrates the processes that learners go through in inferring the meanings of unknown words from reading. To begin with, think aloud the processes you go through, pretending that you are going to infer the word *pigpen* in the following passage.

> It was another hot and humid day at the state fair. My brother wanted to go straight to the rides, but I convinced my family that we should first return to the pigpen. When we got to the arena, there was a crowd again around the mother's pigpen. We waited for our turn to see her more closely. Just like the other day, she was laying there with her seven piglets. She looked a little more exhausted today. Despite what she might be feeling, everyone there was so happy to see the adorable babies.

In word-meaning inference during reading, what you need to do first is to identify a word that you are not familiar with, and then decide to infer the meaning of the unfamiliar word. The example given above is a case of a compound word, in which the word is made up of the two words, *pig* and *pen*. Because both words are at the basic level of vocabulary, you are able to identify the two words (roots) in the word, *pigpen*, but still come to the conclusion that you are not familiar with the word as a whole. What processes are involved when you decide whether a word is familiar or unfamiliar?

When you identify a word, you first need to "decode" the graphic form of the word. Decoding involves converting the written word into its spoken form. The graphic form is the letter string, p-i-g-p-e-n, written in lowercase Roman alphabet. You convert the letter string into its corresponding phonemes, /pɪgpɛn/, and use the phonological information to look up the meaning of the word in your mental lexicon. If you are able to find the meaning during the search, then the word is familiar. If you are not able to find the meaning, then the word is not familiar. It should be noted that word knowledge is not clear-cut "familiar or unfamiliar" (Wesche and Paribakht, 1996). For some words, you may possess partial knowledge, because word learning is incremental.

4.3.2 Making Use of the Information from a Word

During the mental lexicon search, you are able to find the meanings for the word parts, *pig* and *pen*, because these are basic vocabulary that you are familiar with. The meanings you retrieve from the mental lexicon are probably similar to the following: *pen* refers to "a writing instrument that uses ink" and *pig* refers to "a domesticated animal with short legs and produces pork." You are not familiar with the word, *pigpen*, but based on the semantic information you extracted from the word parts, *pig* and *pen*, you are able to infer the meaning of the word. You may think that the word means a kind of pen, probably a pen that has a pig's picture on it. Apparently, word-meaning inference is unsuccessful at this point. What can you do to make it successful?

4.3.3 Integrating the Information from a Text as a Whole

What is missing in the unsuccessful attempt earlier is the use of information other than information from the target word itself. The additional information needed is the contextual information, the information based on comprehension of the text. Contextual information can be generated at any moment as you comprehend the message of a portion of or an entire text. It could be from comprehension of phrases and sentences, or even larger units, such as paragraphs or an entire text. Contextual information can be generated only with accurate reading comprehension. In order to generate contextual information from the example passage, you need to possess basic linguistic skills (vocabulary knowledge, morpho-syntactic knowledge) and apply the skills to various stages of reading processes, such as recognizing the words in the text, parsing individual words into phrases and sentences, and interpreting the message from them. You also need to apply background knowledge, such as knowledge about farm animals and fairs, in order to facilitate the comprehension processes.

With accurate contextual information, you should be able to notice that the meaning you identified for the word, *pen*, does not fit the context. You need to try to infer a different meaning. If you know the other meaning of *pen*, which is "a small enclosure where domestic animals are kept," it is relatively easy. If you don't know the other meaning, then you would have to infer the other meaning based on the contextual information. Only after you infer the other meaning of *pen*, would you be able to infer the accurate meaning of *pigpen*. You may also make use of the sentence-level context to infer the accurate meaning. If *pigpen* is a kind of pen (i.e., a writing instrument), then the sentence that the word belongs to does not make sense, "returned to the *pigpen*." What other sentences can you think of using the verb, *return*? "I returned the money to you," "I returned to my room." It seems that the second sentence sounds similar to the one in the example passage. If you analyze the structure of the sentence, "I returned to my room," you would probably think it doesn't make sense to return to a pen, a writing instrument. The word, *pen*, must mean something other than a writing instrument in the example passage. Based on the sentence-level context, you should be able to realize that you need to re-infer the meaning of *pen*, as well as *pigpen*.

4.4 Introducing the Cognitive Model of Word-Meaning Inference

4.4.1 Overview of the Model

This section proposes the Cognitive Model of Word-Meaning Inference (Figure 4.1), which reflects the processes illustrated in the example passage earlier—what information learners obtain from reading and how they make use of the information for inferring the meanings of unfamiliar words. The model aims to summarize the processes learners go through when inferring the meanings of new words from reading, by incorporating the reading models introduced in this chapter. The currently available models (see Chapter 2) tend to focus on describing the processes or factors only in word learning. The Cognitive Model places equal importance on the processes or factors in both reading and word learning, because success in learning words from reading is dependent upon success in reading.

According to Nation's definition (2001), word knowledge consists of the following three major components: form, meaning, and use (see more in

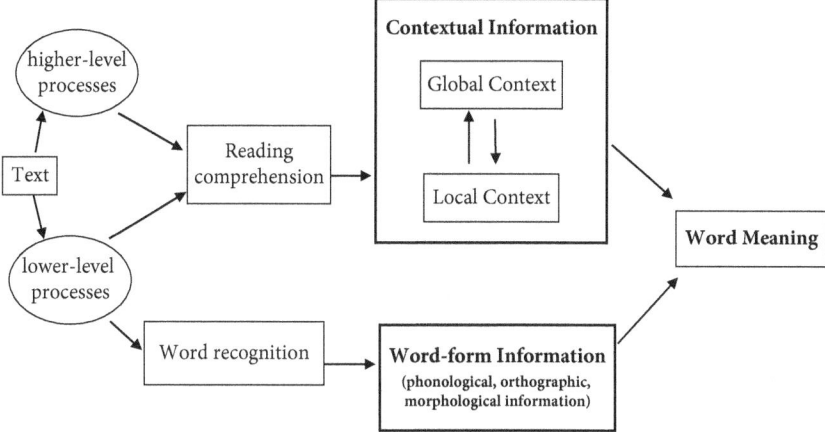

Figure 4.1 Cognitive model of word-meaning inference.

Chapter 2). In learning words from reading, form and use are available in the text. Thus, the primary task is to learn the meanings of the words. There are different ways to learn the meanings, either intentionally through L1 translation or definitions or through inferencing based on the context. The goal of the model is to clarify the processes involved in inferring the meanings of unfamiliar words from L2 reading. It needs to be noted that the connection (or mapping) between different aspects of word knowledge is certainly important in overall word-knowledge development in a second language (e.g., Jiang, 2002), but it is beyond the scope of the model and thus not included. The rest of this section explains each component process in the model.

4.4.2 Word-Form Information and Contextual Information

The model assumes that when learners infer the meanings of words from reading, they make use of two sources of information: word-form information and contextual information. Word-form information is the information originating from the linguistic characteristics of a word, including orthographic information (what letters are in the word, how they look, and how they are sequenced), phonological information (what the word or word parts sound like), and morphological information (what word parts are contained in the word). In learning words from reading, although learners may access the semantic information of the word parts, the semantic information of the word is unknown and that is what they are going to learn by inferencing.

Contextual information is the information based on the messages that learners receive from the text. In the model, contextual information is further categorized into local contextual information and global contextual information, depending on the amount of text that is necessary to generate the contextual information. Local contextual information is generated from understanding of phrase- or sentence-level context, which the word to be inferred belongs to. Global contextual information is generated from understanding of larger units in the text, such as paragraphs or an entire text, with support from prior knowledge and experience learners possess related to the text. In the example passage given earlier, having knowledge of or experience with fairs and farm animals increases the familiarity with the scene and helps generate global contextual information.

4.4.3 Extracting Word-Form Information and Generating Contextual Information

In the model, the processes of obtaining word-form and contextual information are described as extraction and generation. Word-form information is extracted from a word through word recognition processes. For example, identifying that there are three letters, p-e-n, in *pen* is accomplished by extracting the orthographic information from the word; and identifying the suffix, *-able*, in *adorable*, is accomplished by extracting the morphological information from the word. The extraction process is rule-governed and should be straightforward as long as learners possess sufficient linguistic ability.

On the other hand, the generation process is more complex and requires a process unique to a specific text. Learners need to come up with their own conclusions for each specific text, rather than applying a set of rules as in extracting word-form information. To generate local contextual information, they need to integrate the individual words' information into phrases and sentences and interpret them. To generate global contextual information, they need to integrate the interpretation of each sentence into coherent units, such as paragraphs, sections, or chapters. The generation process also involves information beyond what is written in the text. As introduced in the example passage, our background knowledge and experiences also contribute to the generation process. Suppose you saw the following sentence in winter, what message would you receive? "Tomorrow's high is 40° F." If you live in a region that has a warmer climate, you may interpret the sentence as "it will be cold tomorrow." If you live in a region that has a colder climate, you may interpret the sentence as "it will be warm tomorrow." When learners generate contextual information from a text, they are interpreting the text through their own world view, shaped by their experiences.

4.4.4 Dual Processing of Word-Form and Contextual Information

Word-form information is more straightforward to obtain, because the process is less complex than reading comprehension. Because of its simplicity or convenience, learners may infer the meaning of a word based solely on word-form information without making use of contextual information. However, not all word-form information is helpful for word-meaning inference (Nagy, 1997). For example, the meaning of *apartment* cannot be easily inferred from the root, *apart*, and the suffix, *-ment*, as in *entertainment* or *advertisement*. Furthermore, learners may be misled by a mere orthographic resemblance to words they are familiar with. For example, ESL students inferred the meaning of *permeate* as *meat* (Nassaji, 2003a) and the meaning of *enormous* as *normal* (Haynes, 1993). These unsuccessful inferences could have been avoided if the students had also made use of contextual information.

The model assumes that the extraction of word-form information and the generation of contextual information happen simultaneously as learners read a text. However, we cannot expect that all learners are able to obtain both kinds of information accurately and make accurate use of them for word-meaning inference. In fact, research suggests that lower-proficiency students tend to be misled by the word-form information due to a failure to incorporate the contextual information (e.g., Hamada, 2014; Mori and Nagy, 1999). In order to be successful in word-meaning inference, learners need to be able to integrate both word-form and contextual information.

4.4.5 Lower-Level and Higher-Level Processes in Reading

There are two ways to describe the processes involved in reading: higher-level and lower-level processes. The lower-level processes primarily involve the processes in word recognition. For example, learners need to first identify which letters are in the word. After they extract the information of most of the words in a text, they are able to interpret sentences and comprehend the text as a whole. As introduced in the earlier sections, research has suggested that word recognition skills are fundamental for reading comprehension (e.g., Gough, 1972; Stanovich, 1984).

More recently, studies have begun investigating the connection between word recognition and word-meaning inference (e.g., Godfroid, Boers, and Housen, 2013; Pellicer-Sánchez, 2016). There are also some findings suggesting that phonological decoding contributes to word-meaning inference (Brusnighan et al., 2014; Prior et al., 2014). Phonological decoding refers to one aspect of word recognition processes, the process for extracting a word's phonological information (Koda, 2005). Efficient phonological decoding enables learners to extract phonological information more efficiently (accurately and fast), which is expected to help them create a stronger mental representation of the word whose meaning is to be inferred.

Higher-level processes involve the processes of integrating the information extracted through the lower-level processes. For example, learners integrate words into phrases and sentences and interpret the meanings. They then integrate the meanings of phrases and sentences into larger units, such as paragraphs and entire texts, and understand the messages from the texts by incorporating the textual meanings with their background knowledge.

4.4.6 Word Recognition to Word-Form Information to Word-Meaning Inference

Word recognition processes enable learners to identify words. This includes the identification of both known words and unknown words. Identification of unknown words provides the learners with words whose meanings they are going to infer if they choose to do so. If they misrecognize a word as "known," then word-meaning inference does not happen. In order to recognize words, they need to access lexical information in their mental lexicon. Lexical information includes orthographic information, phonological information, morphological information, and semantic information.

For known words, learners should be able to access all four aspects of lexical information. For unknown words, they are not able to access the semantic information because it is absent from their mental lexicon. If they decide to infer the meanings of the unknown words, they need to use the phonological, orthographic, and morphological information that they extracted through word recognition processes. These three pieces of information are referred to as word-form information in the model. Note that morphological information includes the semantic information of word parts. The word-form information also serves as a label for the unknown words, so that learners are able to revisit the words to continue working on inferring their meanings.

4.4.7 Reading Comprehension to Contextual Information to Word-Meaning Inference

Reading comprehension provides contextual information, which learners make use of for inferring word meanings. As mentioned earlier, reading involves interactive processes. Comprehension of individual phrases and sentences is necessary for the comprehension of larger units, such as paragraphs and an entire text, and comprehension of larger units or the main point of a text helps to understand the sentence-level meanings. In other words, the global level of comprehension is interdependent with the local level of comprehension. Similarly, in word-meaning inference, the generation of local and global contextual information are interdependent with each other. The global contextual information generated from the larger units influences the generation of local contextual information, and vice versa.

4.5 Chapter Summary

The first half of this chapter summarized the cognitive models of reading processes and introduced theories specific to L2 reading. These models and theories provided a theoretical ground for the Cognitive Model of Word-Meaning Inference proposed in the second half of this chapter. The Cognitive Model aims to explain the connection between reading and word-meaning inference by identifying the shared processes between them. Learners obtain word-form and contextual information from a text and make use of the information for inferring the meanings of unknown words encountered in the text.

In learning an L2, learners' L1 linguistic background is a factor that cannot be ignored. Cross-linguistic transfer influences virtually all aspects of L2 learning, and reading is not an exception to its influence. As introduced earlier in this chapter, L2 reading involves dual-language processing. The processes that learners employ in L2 reading differ according to the similarities and differences between L1 and L2 linguistic structures (e.g., writing system, morpho-syntactic system) and other related factors (e.g., cultural norms, discourse structure). As learners achieve higher proficiency in L2, their reading processes are refined and they may gradually start using processes that resemble native speakers' processes.

As much as cross-linguistic transfer influences reading, the Cognitive Model proposed in this chapter acknowledges that cross-linguistic transfer influences word-meaning inference as well. In each of the components in the model, cross-linguistic transfer influences the ways in which the component is processed. As a result, both kinds of information, the word-form information that learners extract through word recognition and the contextual information they generate through reading comprehension, are subject to the influence of cross-linguistic transfer. In order to explain how word-form information is extracted and contextual information is generated, the next two chapters summarize the processes involved in word recognition and sentence and text comprehension.

5

Extracting Word-Form Information

The Cognitive Model of Word-Meaning Inference asserts that learners make use of word-form information for inferring the meanings of unknown words encountered during reading. Word-form information includes the orthographic, phonological, and morphological information of a word, which is extracted through word recognition processes. For a better understanding of word recognition processes, the first section of this chapter summarizes the word recognition theories and models based on the findings from L1 readers. The section aims to clarify the processes through which we extract word-form information, including cross-linguistic variation of the processes. The second section of the chapter summarizes the findings from L2 word recognition studies, introducing cross-linguistic transfer in L2 word recognition. Cross-linguistic transfer that affects L2 word recognition processes can influence the ways in which learners extract word-form information for inferring the meanings of unknown words. The second section also addresses possible consequences of cross-linguistic transfer on word-meaning inference.

5.1 Word Recognition Theories and Models

5.1.1 What Is Written Language?

Which city were you born in? What language or languages did your caregivers use? What language(s) did you speak when you were growing up? If you had been born in a different country or city or to caregivers who used a different language, what language do you think you would have started speaking? All humans who are born with normal cognitive ability and raised in a normal environment are able to communicate with other people using the language(s) spoken in the environment in which they grow up, without receiving formal instruction. Oral language acquisition happens naturally, which makes humans distinct from other living creatures.

Written language acquisition is not as natural as oral language acquisition. For many of us who are fluent readers, reading seems effortless and as natural as listening. However, written language acquisition does not happen in the same manner as oral language acquisition. Written language acquisition necessitates deliberate learning, which can include formal instruction. Unlike oral language, written language is a human creation, and in fact, not all languages have written scripts. Because written language is an invention, we need to decipher the written scripts in order to make sense of what they mean, just like musical notes or street signs. The invention of written language has changed our society drastically. Wolf (2007: 3) states that after the invention of written language, we "rearranged the very organization of our brain, which in turn expanded the ways we were able to think." The fact that written language is an invention means it requires us to make conscious effort to become able to read.

5.1.2 Written Language Represents Spoken Language

Why did we, humans, invent written language? The main benefit is probably the ability to preserve information for audiences in different times and locations. We take notes for many activities (e.g., shopping, study). These notes help us remember things that are important in the activities. Written language also helps us gain new knowledge. For example, reading helps us learn about things that happened in the past in a different location we have never visited. Without written language, we would need to use an audio recorder to preserve information and have access to it. Having a written version of the information is certainly more convenient.

In understanding word recognition processes, it is important to clarify what kind of linguistic information is preserved in written language. The essential role of written language is to record oral language in a written form. A good example is phonetic spelling. Beginning-level learners may spell "kandee" for *candy*. We may spell "U" for *you* when we send a text message. These invented spellings represent how the messages should sound when they are read aloud, and we understand the messages even though the words are not spelled correctly. Reading is sometimes referred to as cracking a code, because our task is to convert written language into a format that is understandable (spoken language).

The universal grammar of reading (Perfetti, 2003; Perfetti, Liu, and Tan, 2005) explains the fundamentals of written language and reading using the following two principles: the language constraint on writing systems and the universal phonological principle. The first principle asserts the fundamental relationship between written language and spoken language. Written symbols represent spoken language, and the relationship between written and spoken language is language universal. However, the way that spoken language is mapped onto written language is language specific, dependent on the writing system and orthography that a language employs. The second principle reiterates the fundamental relationship between written and spoken language in the context of reading. The essential task we have to complete when we read is to convert the written code into spoken language. This principle states that phonological information is activated in reading and its activation occurs in all languages. In order to become fluent in reading, we need to be able to crack the code effortlessly and accurately—this is the process referred to as decoding or phonological decoding.

The automatic activation of phonological information in reading can be observed an experimental task in word recognition, the Stroop task (Stroop, 1935). In the task, research participants are asked to say aloud the ink color of color words as quickly as possible. When the ink color matches the word, their responses are quicker and free from error. In contrast, when the ink color does not match the word (e.g., the word, *red*, written with green ink), their responses are typically slower and more erroneous. The difficulty in the mismatched condition comes from the activation of phonological information that is difficult to suppress. Reading involves a transformation of written symbols into spoken language, which happens automatically.

5.1.3 Writing System

The writing system of a language determines how spoken language is mapped onto written symbols. There are three types of writing systems: alphabetic, syllabic, and logographic systems, summarized in Figure 5.1.

In an alphabetic writing system, letters represent phonemes. For example, in the English word, *cat*, each letter represents the sounds /k/ /æ/ /t/, respectively.

Writing System	Mapping of "cat" between spoken and written language
Alphabetic	English 'cat' c a t | | \ /k/ /æ/ /t/
Syllabic	Japanese Hiragana 'ねこ' ね こ | \ /nɛ/ /ko/
Logographic	Japanese Kanji ' 猫' 猫 | /nɛko/

Figure 5.1 Characteristics of writing systems.

In a syllabic writing system, letters represent syllables. For example, in the Japanese equivalent of *cat*, ねこ, written in Hiragana script, the first letter, ね, represents the syllable /nɛ/ and the second letter こ, represents the syllable /ko/. In a logographic writing system, each symbol (also called a character) represents a morpheme. For example, the Japanese equivalent of *cat*, written in Kanji script, is 猫, and this entire symbol represents the meaning of *cat* and the sounds of /nɛko/. Unlike alphabetic and syllabic writing systems, there is no phonological segmentation in the character.

5.1.4 Orthography and the Orthographic Depth Hypothesis

Each language has its unique orthographic system. Orthography describes more specific rules in which spoken language is mapped onto the graphic symbols for the language. Orthographic depth indicates the degree of correspondence between spoken language and written language, primarily within languages that employ an alphabetic writing system (Frost, Katz, and Bentin, 1987). Languages can be classified as having either a transparent (shallow) or an opaque (deep) orthography. If a language has more one-to-one letter-phoneme (grapheme-phoneme) correspondences and very few exceptional spellings, then the language has a transparent orthographic system.

If a language has more one-to-many grapheme-phoneme correspondences and more irregular spellings, such as *aisle* in English, the language has an opaque orthographic system. For example, in Spanish, the letter "a" represents one sound, /a/, whereas in English, the same letter represents multiple sounds,

/æ/ as in "man," /eɪ/ as in "ace," and /ɛ/ as in "fare." Another example is the English past tense morpheme. The graphemes are *ed*, but it is pronounced in three different ways, as in "*talked*" [t], "*visited*" [ɪd], and "*called*" [d]. Arabic and Hebrew employ an unvowelized orthography, in which some vowels are omitted in a text written for normal adult audiences. An unvowelized version of English would look like "kck (kick)" and "lmp (lamp)." The fact that the entire spoken language is not represented in the written symbols is the reason why these two languages are placed at the most opaque end of the orthographic depth spectrum (see Perfetti and Dunlap, 2008).

5.1.5 Development of Word Recognition Skills

Literacy researchers have proposed various theories to explain the development of word recognition skills among young children. One of the earlier theories by Gough and Juel (1991) suggests that the first stage of word recognition is carried out by selective association, in which children select a cue from a word and use it to recognize the word. They are not necessarily paying attention to the word itself, but instead pick up a cue that helps them connect the written word to its spoken form. For example, the cue might be the word's color, length, or resemblance to a familiar object. After this stage, children transition to the cipher stage, in which they start using the knowledge of grapheme-phoneme correspondences to recognize words.

Similarly, Ehri (1995, 1998) suggests that the development of grapheme-phoneme correspondences, called the alphabetic principle, is critical for the development of word recognition skills and explains that there are four phases in the development of English word recognition skills. In the pre-alphabetic phase, children associate a graphic cue with a word, and use the cue to recognize the word. For example, in recognizing the word, *look*, children may use the graphic features of the two o's as the cue because they resemble eyes (oo). At this phase, children do not yet have the knowledge of grapheme-phoneme correspondences. In the second phase, the partial alphabetic phase, children associate only some of the letters with their corresponding sounds to recognize the word. For example, in recognizing the word, *cat*, they may associate the first and the last letters with their corresponding phonemes (c for /k/ and t for /t/). Children at this phase may spell LFT for the word, *elephant*, or JRF for the word, *giraffe*, by picking up some of the letter-sound correspondences of the word. In the third phase, the full alphabetic phase, children are able to apply their knowledge of grapheme-phoneme correspondences to recognize the word (e.g., c for /k/, a for /æ/, and t for /t/). In the fourth phase, the consolidated alphabetic phase, children connect graphemes to phonemes at a larger unit, onset and rhyme ("c" for /k/ and "at" for /æt/), because onsets and rhymes have more consistent grapheme-phoneme correspondences in English.

The psycholinguistic grain size theory (Ziegler and Goswami, 2005, 2006) further explains how variations in writing system and orthography influence the development of word recognition skills. Although the theory was developed based on research with native-speaking children, it has also been confirmed by studies with bilingual children and ESL learners (e.g., Gottardo et al., 2016). According to the theory, children initially develop sensitivity to larger phonological units in speech, such as morphemes or syllables, but gradually become able to distinguish smaller units. The size of the phonological unit required for processing a language is determined by the amount of graphic information suitable for phonological information extraction in the language.

For example, within an alphabetic writing system with a more transparent orthography, such as Finnish, individual graphemes are mapped onto phonemes in a regular and consistent manner without exceptions. A child may initially process entire words (e.g., *cat*) holistically without any segmentation, but will eventually develop the skill to map one grapheme to one phoneme (e.g., c for /k/, a for /æ/, and t for /t/). In English, a child may initially process entire words holistically, but will eventually develop the skill to map onsets and rhymes to their respective sounds (e.g., "c" for /k/ and "at" for /æt/) because there is higher grapheme-phoneme consistency at the onset and the rhyme units in English. In Arabic or Hebrew, children's texts typically include all of the vowels, although the letters for short vowels are absent in adult texts. Therefore, as in Finnish and English, a child may initially process entire words, but will eventually develop the skill to map a consonantal root to its respective sound.

In a logographic writing system, Chinese and Japanese Kanji, there is no phonological segmentation in mapping. The whole sound of the word, *cat*, is mapped onto the symbol that represents the sound. Some of the symbols, called characters, are made up of word parts, which contain the semantic and phonetic information of the characters. For example, the following characters, 海 (ocean), 湖 (lake), and 池 (pond), all contain a radical, 氵, which indicates the meaning of "water." The following characters, 精 (spirit), 晴 (cloudless), and 請 (to request, implore) include 青 and have the same pronunciation, /sɛɪ/.

5.1.6 Role of Word Recognition in Reading Comprehension

Are individual words important in reading? During the 1970s and 1980s, a time when the top-down approach to reading was more prevalent, it was believed that readers did not need to pay attention to individual words in a text. Reading was viewed as a psycholinguistic guessing game (Goodman, 1967, 1970), and the readers were supposed to hypothesize what a text should mean based on their own view. The information in the text was used merely to confirm the hypothesis, rather than being the main source of information for understanding the text. Under this approach, building word recognition skills was not considered to be crucial for literacy development. It was expected that children would become able to read naturally through exposure to a print-rich environment, surrounded by books and other written materials.

The top-down approach began to be viewed skeptically when eye movement research was introduced. Eye movement research uses an eye tracker to record eye fixation data, that is, data regarding where the eyes are focused on and how long the eyes remain in a particular position. Research with native speakers of English indicated that fluent readers looked at almost all of the words in the text (Carpenter and Just, 1983; Just and Carpenter, 1980). Accurate reading comprehension is accomplished not from guessing but from retrieving information from individual words in the text. Word recognition has come to be regarded as an integral component of reading development, and a more systematic approach for teaching grapheme-phoneme correspondences has started to be implemented in early reading instruction.

5.1.7 Word Recognition Models

The dual route model (Coltheart, 1980) proposes that there are two routes in visual word recognition: the addressed phonology route (lexical route) and the assembled phonology route (non-lexical route). The model was originally established based on data from a naming task, in which participants were shown a string of letters, either an existing word or a pseudoword (a non-existing but orthographically permissible word), and asked to read it aloud as quickly and accurately as possible. Their pronunciation (how they read) and reaction time (the time between the onset of the letter-string presentation and the onset of the voice) were recorded as data. A faster reaction time and more accurate pronunciation meant that the letter string was recognized more easily. The dual-route model was subsequently developed into a computational model, the dual-route cascaded (DRC) model (Coltheart et al., 2001).

In the addressed phonology route (lexical route), readers look at the entire word (e.g., the letter string "cat") and connect the word to its corresponding phonological information. In order to find the phonological information of the word, they need to know the semantic information of the word as well, that is, they need to have knowledge of the word. For example, in recognizing a word that has exceptional and irregular grapheme-phoneme correspondences, such as *aisle*, readers need to know what the word should mean and sound like, because if it was read phonetically, it would not sound like the word they know. Because semantic access happens at about the same time as phonological access, addressed phonology is also referred to as lexical phonology.

In the assembled phonology route (non-lexical route), the word is segmented and decoded into corresponding phonemes (c /k/, a /æ/, t /t/), and after all of the phonemes are decoded, they are assembled into the phonological information (pronunciation) of the word. In this route, phonological access is a more rule-based process, and readers use their knowledge of grapheme-phoneme correspondences to decode letters into phonemes. The semantic access happens after the phonological information is retrieved. Because the phonological processing precedes the semantic processing, assembled phonology is also referred to as prelexical phonology.

The connectionist model, proposed by Seidenberg and McClelland (1989), is another important word recognition model, which was developed based on the premise that language learning is a result of strong associations in neural networks in the brain. It is a computational model that describes the processes involved in reading words aloud and is also referred to as the triangle model (e.g., Harm and Seidenberg, 2004; Perry, Ziegler, and Zorzi, 2007). The model is often referred to as a "single route" model, in comparison to the dual-route model, yet this common claim is deemed wrong (Coltheart, 2007). In the model, three components (orthography, phonology, and semantics) operate as independent components, and there are two pathways from written words to their sounds: the direct pathway (orthography to phonology) and the pathway via semantics. For example, when readers are presented with the written word, "make," in the pathway via phonology, they reach the word's phonological information (/meɪk/) by converting graphemes into phonemes. In the pathway via semantics, the readers search the word as a whole in the mental lexicon. Once they find the word, its lexical information, including semantic and phonological information, becomes available. When the connection within one pathway is strengthened by repeated activation, then that pathway gets to be chosen over the other.

The connectionist model and dual-route model have also shown that there are some word-inherent factors that influence word recognition processes. Word frequency is one of them. Word frequency is determined by statistical calculation of how commonly a word is seen in print in comparison to other words. In the dual-route model, high frequency words are expected to be processed through the addressed phonology route. If readers encounter the same words repeatedly, they do not need to process the entire letter string in a linear manner. For example, in reading this book, you may see the word *linguistics* so many times that you do not conduct a grapheme-phoneme conversion for each letter while reading. In the connectionist model, higher frequency words create a stronger connection within the neural network from repeated activation. Therefore, readers become able to recognize the meanings of higher frequency words through the route from orthography to semantics, without going through phonological mediation.

Regularity and consistency of grapheme-phoneme correspondences is also a factor that influences word recognition processes. As explained earlier, words that have more regular and consistent grapheme-phoneme correspondences, such as *cat*, are typically recognized using the assembled phonology route in the dual-route model. On the other hand, words that have more exceptional grapheme-phoneme correspondences, such as *aisle*, are recognized using the addressed phonology route, because these words would be misrecognized if they were accessed through the assembled phonology route. The phonological information of exceptional words needs to be retrieved from the addressed phonology route.

It should be noted that the two models, connectionist and dual route, mainly describe the recognition of words that have a simple structure. How are words that contain multiple word parts (e.g., *helpful*, *carwash*) recognized? The recognition of morphologically complex words necessitates an additional step, in which readers recognize word-part information. For instance, in recognizing the word, *carwash*, readers may decompose the word into parts, *car* and *wash*, before accessing the meaning of the word. Alternatively, in recognizing the word, *hogwash*, readers access the word's meaning without decomposing it. The model proposed by Verhoeven and Perfetti (2011) incorporates the two possibilities for accessing a word's meaning, morphological decomposition and direct access to the word as a single orthographic unit.

5.2 Cross-Linguistic Transfer during the Extraction of Word-Form Information

5.2.1 Where in a Word Do Learners Pay More Attention?

In recognizing a written word, the tendency to look at a particular location within a word can cause misrecognition, which can influence the quality of word-form information extracted during word recognition. For example, Green and Meara (1987) used a letter search task to examine cross-linguistic variations in letter identification between native speakers of English and advanced ESL students (Arabic L1, Chinese L1, and Spanish L1). In the task, the students were first shown a single letter (e.g., *S*). Immediately after the letter presentation, a five-letter string (e.g., *SPOAG*) was shown, and they identified whether the letter was included in the string. The results indicated that native speakers of English and Spanish L1 ESL learners were most efficient (fast and accurate) in identifying the letter when it was in the left-most position. In contrast, both the Arabic L1 and Chinese L1 ESL learners were most efficient in identifying the letter if it was in the middle position, demonstrating the same patterns as when they performed the task in their L1s. For the Chinese L1 ESL learners, the results reflected how Chinese characters were recognized without linear segmentation, but the Arabic L1 ESL learners' results did not indicate strength in the right-most letter, following the direction of Arabic writing, although there was a slight trend toward the right.

Subsequent studies reported similar findings demonstrating the influence of L1 orthographic systems on L2 letter identification (Green, Meara, and Court, 1989; Liow, Green, and Tam, 1999; Randall and Meara, 1988). Furthermore,

Hamada (2017) found similar patterns in cross-linguistic differences in the recognition of a longer letter string (nine letters) with three syllables (e.g., *cutmigdaw*). Both Arabic L1 and Chinese L1 ESL learners were most efficient in identifying the left-most syllable, demonstrating the same position preference as native speakers of English. However, the Arabic L1 ESL learners also showed a higher sensitivity to the right-most syllable than the other two participant groups.

5.2.2 Misled by a Semantically and Morphologically Unrelated Letter String

In extracting word-form information, some learners are misled by a letter string that looks or sounds similar to a word they know. For instance, Haynes (1993) reported that college-level ESL students inferred the meaning of *habitat* as "being used to something" (related to *habit*) and the meaning of *crept* as "some kind of pancake" (related to *crepe*). Likewise, Nassaji (2003a) found that college-level ESL students inferred the meaning of *permeated* and *affluence* as related to *meat* and *influence*, respectively. This type of error was attributed to the use of word-form analogy, in which the students treated a letter string as if it was morphologically and semantically related to the meaning of the word.

It may appear that the use of analogy is a behavior specific to L2 learners. However, research has reported that orthographic similarities interfere with word recognition even among fluent L1 readers (e.g., Bowers, Davis, and Hanley, 2005a, 2005b; Duñabeitia, Carreiras, and Perea, 2008; Nation and Cocksey, 2009). Bowers, Davis, and Hanley (2005a) asked English L1 college students to judge whether a word belonged to a semantic category. For instance, the students saw a word (e.g., *hatch*) and judged whether the word belonged to a category, such as, "item of clothing" or "human body part." Their responses were slower and less accurate when an embedded word (e.g., *hat* in <u>hat</u>ch) matched the category. If orthographic information is activated during word recognition even for fluent L1 readers, it seems unavoidable that L2 learners would make use of word-form analogy in word learning from reading. Given that word-form analogy almost always leads to inaccurate meanings, learners need to integrate and evaluate both word-form information and contextual information in order to succeed in word-meaning inference.

5.2.3 Sensitivity to Orthographic and Phonological Information

Depending on L1 writing system and orthography, some learners may be more skilled at extracting orthographic information from a word, while others may be more skilled at extracting phonological information. Their sensitivity to either orthographic or phonological information can influence the word-form information they extract during word recognition. A number of studies have suggested that L2 learners with an alphabetic L1 script background (e.g., Korean, Persian, Spanish, Russian) are more sensitive to the phonological information of a word, while L2 learners with a logographic L1 orthographic background (Chinese, Japanese) are more sensitive to the orthographic information of a word (e.g., Akamatsu, 2003; Brown and Haynes, 1985; Wang and Koda, 2005; Wang, Koda, and Perfetti, 2003).

For instance, Wang, Koda, and Perfetti (2003) used a semantic category judgment task to measure the impact of L1 orthographic transfer in L2 word recognition. In the study, Korean L1 ESL learners and Chinese L1 ESL learners were first presented with a category description, such as "flower" or "body part," and then decided whether a target word was a member of the given category. The target word was either phonologically similar (e.g., "rows" for "rose") or graphically similar (e.g., "fees" for "feet") to a word that belongs to the category. The Korean L1 ESL learners falsely accepted the phonologically similar target more often than the graphically similar target, which was consistent with the findings with native-speaking English participants (van Orden, 1987). In contrast, the Chinese L1 ESL learners showed the opposite pattern, falsely accepting the graphically similar target more often. Moreover, Hamada and Koda (2011) found the same patterns of sensitivity in L2 word learning. They found that Chinese L1 ESL students were better at remembering the orthographic information of the target words, while Korean L1 ESL learners were better at remembering the phonological information of the target words.

5.2.4 Difficulty in Recognizing Letters That Represent Vowels

As introduced earlier, Arabic is one of the languages that employ an unvowelized script. Short vowels, /i/ /u/ and /ɑ/, are omitted from normal texts for adult audiences, because these vowels usually provide functional information (e.g., tense, number) and can be inferred from context (Hayes-Harb, 2006). Because of the absence of vowel letters, context plays an important role in reading in Arabic (Abu Rabia, 1995, 1997). The primary information comes from a consonantal root, which provides the morphological information of a word. For example, k-t-b is the root that indicates the meaning of "writing," such as kitaab (book), kataba (he wrote), and maktaba (library). Fluent readers are able to fill in the correct vowels in the root according to the context.

If learners are used to recognizing words written with mainly consonants in their L1, they may experience difficulty extracting letters that represent vowels. Hayes-Harb (2006) and Ryan and Meara (1991) used an identity judgment task to examine the influence of Arabic L1 orthographic experience in English L2 word recognition. In the task, college-level ESL learners were asked to indicate whether two consecutively presented words were identical. In the identical condition, the first and second words were spelled identically, whereas in the deleted vowel condition, a vowel was missing from the second word (e.g., department—dpartment). The results indicated that Arabic L1 ESL learners were slower and less accurate in the task, compared to ESL learners with other L1 backgrounds. Similarly, Saigh and Schmitt (2012) demonstrated that college-level Arabic L1 ESL learners had difficulty identifying misspellings of vowels in sentences, such as "monky" for *monkey* (missing letter) and "hobet" for *habit* (wrong letters). Misrecognition of vowels can have a negative impact on the extraction of word-form information and subsequent word-meaning inference.

5.2.5 Misrecognizing Words That Include a Phoneme That Doesn't Exist in L1

It is commonly known that L1 phonological transfer influences L2 speaking and listening performance. L2 learners often have difficulty pronouncing or hearing phonemes that do not exist in their L1 phonemic inventory. Although reading does not involve the same degree of phonological processing required in oral language, reading does involve phonological processing, mostly performed silently, as explained at the beginning of this chapter. Readers have to convert written scripts into their sounds (or oral language), which fluent readers usually do silently in their head.

A number of studies have reported that L1 phonological transfer occurs in L2 visual word recognition as well. For example, Ota, Hartsuiker, and

Haywood (2009) used a semantic relatedness decision task in order to compare L1 phonological transfer between Arabic L1 ESL and Japanese L1 ESL students. In the task, the learners saw a set of two words and determined whether their meanings were related. For the Arabic L1 ESL students, the targeted phonemic contrast was the letters *p* and *b*, because the phoneme /p/ does not exist in their L1 but the phoneme /b/ does. For the Japanese L1 ESL learners, the targeted phonemic contrast was the letters *l* and *r*, because the phoneme /ɹ/ does not exist in their L1 but the phoneme /l/ does. As predicted, the Arabic L1 and Japanese L1 ESL learners did not distinguish between the targeted letters and treated the contrasting letters as if they were identical. For example, the Japanese L1 ESL learners falsely determined the combination of KEY-ROCK as semantically related, treating rock and lock as if they were synonymous. Similar findings were reported in ESL studies with various L1s, such as Hebrew (Wade-Woolley and Geva, 2000), Spanish (Ota, Hartsuiker, and Haywood, 2010), and Russian (Shafiro and Kharkhurin, 2009). Misrecognition of words caused by L1 phonological transfer can impact the word-form information that learners extract for subsequent word-meaning inference.

5.2.6 Preferred Phonological and Orthographic Structures

Learners are able to process L2 words with phonological and orthographic structures that are similar to their L1s more easily than L2 words with structures dissimilar to their L1s. For example, Muljani, Koda, and Moates (1998) found that L1 phonological transfer extended to a unit larger than single phonemes. In their study, Chinese L1 and Indonesian L1 ESL students performed a lexical decision (identifying whether a letter string was a word) task. The letter strings they identified included both real words and pseudowords with one of the following syllable structures: (C)V(C) (e.g., *galden*) and (C)CCVC(C) (e.g., *trusk*), where C denotes a consonant, V denotes a vowel, and consonants in parentheses are optional. The Indonesian L1 ESL learners performed better in the (C)V(C) condition than the other condition, while the Chinese L1 ESL learners did not show a significant difference between the two syllable structures. Indonesian employs an alphabetic writing system, and the (C)V(C) syllable structure is more common in the language. In contrast, Chinese employs a logographic writing system. The Indonesian L1 ESL learners' preference for the (C)V(C) structure was attributed to the transfer of their L1 syllable structures.

Tremblay (2008) investigated whether L1 prosodic features, in particular, stress patterns, would transfer to L2 word recognition. In Canadian French, stress typically falls on the word-final position, whereas in English, stress can fall on different syllables. In the study, college-level French-speaking ESL learners heard a sentence that ended with a word whose final syllable(s) were missing. Following the listening, they were shown the word options and determined the final word. For example, the learners heard a sentence, "Very few still remember the MYS-" and determined whether the final word in the sentence was one with stress on the first syllable (e.g., *MYStery*) or a word with stress on the second syllable (e.g., *misTAKE*). The learners with lower L2 proficiency had difficulty determining the correct word to complete the sentence, confirming that learners' L1 stress patterns transfer to L2 word recognition.

Bartolotti and Marian (2017) examined the transfer of L1 orthographic structure to L2 word learning. In their study, English L1 college students learned pairs of pictures and pseudowords presented on a computer screen. The pseudowords had two conditions, a wordlike condition (e.g., *baft*) and an unwordlike condition (e.g., *cisv*). The results demonstrated that the students performed better in the wordlike condition. Likewise, Bordag et al. (2017) found that German L2 students learned pseudowords with a high orthographic probability (e.g., *Pend*) more successfully than pseudowords with a low orthographic probability (e.g., *Wrix*) in an intentional-learning condition (see also Chapter 3).

5.2.7 Phonological Processing and Phonological Short-Term Memory

Working memory is a temporary memory system in our brain that enables us to perform various cognitive activities (see more in Chapter 4). Reading and word-meaning inference necessitate the processing of multiple aspects of linguistic information, and the processing is facilitated by working memory. Although there are two encoding systems (phonological and visual), research has repeatedly shown that the phonological loop is more critical in facilitating short-term retention of newly learned words both in L1 and L2 (e.g., Ellis and

Beaton, 1993; Gathercole et al., 1999; Papagno, Valentine, and Baddeley, 1991; Service and Kohonen, 1995).

Regarding the extraction of phonological information, there seem to be cross-linguistic differences in the types of words learners find easier or more difficult. For instance, Koda (1989) reported that Arabic L1 and Spanish L1 ESL students recalled letter strings that were easy to pronounce (e.g., *CAIS*) more successfully than letter strings that were difficult to pronounce (e.g., *XJWZ*). The decreased recall for the difficult letter strings was attributed to the difficulty of extracting phonological information from the strings. In contrast, Japanese L1 ESL students performed equally in both types of letter strings, demonstrating that they could extract phonological information more holistically, presumably due to their L1 logographic experience. Similarly, Hamada and Koda (2008) found that Korean L1 ESL learners were more affected by pronounceability of words in word recognition and word recall than their Chinese L1 counterparts.

5.2.8 Cross-Linguistic Transfer in Extracting Morphological Information

In extracting morphological information from a word, learners have to analyze the morphological structure of the word and identify the word parts. As introduced earlier in this chapter, this process is referred to as morphological decomposition. In reading in L1, researchers seem to agree that decomposition occurs during word recognition (e.g., Fowler, Napps, and Feldman, 1985), yet in L2, it seems there are cross-linguistic variations (e.g., Silva and Clahsen, 2008; Vainio, Pajunen, and Hyönä, 2014). For instance, Vainio, Pajunen, and Hyönä (2014) compared lexical decision performance with three participant groups: Chinese L1 learners of Finnish, Russian L1 learners of Finnish, and native speakers of Finnish. Both Finnish and Russian use inflectional morphemes, where semantic roles are case marked, whereas Chinese does not use inflections. The Finnish words used in the study differed in morphological complexity, including a simple type (a root morpheme), such as *koulu* "school" (nominative singular), and a more complex type (a root + a case marker), such as *kengä+n* "shoe+genitive marker" (genitive singular). The results indicated that lexical decision was faster in the simple type than the more complex type for the Russian L1 and native-speaking groups, while the difference was absent for the Chinese L1 group. The results demonstrated that the Chinese L1 participants did not engage in morphological decomposition as much as the other two groups due to L1 morphological transfer.

Moreover, literacy research suggests that there are cross-linguistic variations in morphological awareness. Morphological awareness is an aspect of metalinguistic awareness, which develops naturally through exposure to a language. Morphological awareness refers to "the ability to parse words and analyze constituent morphemes for the purpose of constructing meaning" (Carlisle, 2000: 170) and plays an important role in literacy skill development. For example, Zhang et al. (2012) found that Chinese readers were more skilled at identifying grammatical structures in compound words than English readers in a structural analogy task, in which the readers judged the similarities between compound words, such as *sunroof, sunrise,* and *sunlight* (*sunroof* and *sunlight* consist of a noun and a noun, whereas *sunrise* consists of a noun and a verb). The researchers explained that the stronger morphological awareness of compounds among the Chinese readers was due to the higher proportion of compounds in Chinese than in English. Likewise, Ramirez et al. (2011) found that Chinese L1 learners of English, ranging from fourth to seventh grades, performed better in a morphological awareness task with compounds than their Spanish L1 counterparts, while Spanish L1 learners of English in the same grades scored higher on a morphological awareness task with derived words.

The head structure of compounds is another morphological factor subject to cross-linguistic transfer. A compound usually has a head morpheme, and the rest of the morphemes serve as modifiers to describe or add more explanation related to the head. English employs an endocentric structure, where the first constituent serves as the modifier and the second constituent as the head. For example, *bookcase* is a type of *case*, not a type of *book*. If a learner's L1 employs a head structure that is different from the L2, it can be difficult for them to learn new compounds. In fact, Nicoladis (1999, 2002) reported that French-English bilingual children produced English compounds with the modifier and head in reversed order, such as *brush-teeth* for *tooth-brush*, applying the French compound structure (the head is the first constituent). Similar results were reported in Foroodi-Nejad and Paradis (2009) with Persian-English bilingual children.

5.2.9 Semantic Transparency: How Useful Are the Morphemes?

Although morphological information is necessary for word-meaning inference, some morphemes provide misleading information that is unrelated to the meaning of the word. Nagy (1997) explains that seemingly consistent compounds can pose great difficulty in learning words from reading. The semantic characteristics of morphologically complex words are explained by semantic transparency (see more in Chapter 3). Semantically transparent words contain morphemes that provide meanings related to the words, whereas semantically opaque words contain morphemes that provide meanings that are remotely related or unrelated to the words.

Nagy and Anderson (1984) classified the semantic transparency of morphologically complex words into the following six degrees, shown with some examples and their immediate ancestors in parentheses: SEM 0 redness (red), SEM 1 hunter (hunt), SEM 2 gunner (gun), SEM 3 password (pass), SEM 4 apartment (apart), SEM 5 dog-days (dog). In the classification, SEM 0 is the most transparent, and SEM 5 is the most opaque. For example, it is straightforward to infer the meaning of *redness* from *red*, while it is not possible infer the meaning of *dog-days* from *dog*. The more opaque a morpheme is, the more misleading it is when learners make use of it for word-meaning inference.

In recognizing compounds, earlier research assumed that morphological decomposition occurs only for semantically transparent compounds (e.g., Sandra, 1990). For example, a semantically transparent compound, *bookshelf*, is decomposed into *book* and *shelf*, in order to access the meaning of the whole word, whereas a semantically opaque compound, *hogwash*, is processed as a whole word without decomposition because accessing the constituents' meanings would lead to the wrong meaning of the compound. However, recent findings suggest that the lexical information of compound constituents can be activated even for semantically opaque compounds both in L1 (e.g., Libben et al., 2003) and L2 (e.g., Li, Jiang, and Gor, 2017). For instance, Li, Jiang, and Gor (2017) found that Chinese ESL learners showed sensitivity to the constituents in semantically transparent compounds (e.g., *tooth* in *toothbrush*) as well as in semantically opaque compounds (e.g., *honey* in *honeymoon*). In order to succeed in word-meaning inference, learners need to be able to suppress or ignore the meanings of semantically opaque constituents while incorporating contextual information.

5.2.10 Are All Semantically Transparent Compounds Easier to Learn?

The previous section argues that word-meaning inference of semantically opaque compounds is more challenging because learners cannot rely on morphological information as they do for semantically transparent compounds. Nevertheless, inferring the meanings of semantically transparent compounds can also pose difficulty. One factor is L1 lexicalization of L2 compounds (whether the compound exists in learners' L1). For example, *honeybee* exists both in English and Korean, but *bankbook* does not exist in Korean. On the other hand, the compound, *eyewater,* exists in Korean, but its equivalent is *tears* (not a compound) in English. Ko, Wang, and Kim (2011) found that college-level Korean L1 ESL learners were better at recognizing English compounds that had an equivalent compound in their L1 (e.g., *honeybee*). Similar results were reported for Chinese-English bilingual children (Cheng, Wang, and Perfetti, 2011).

Another factor that makes the meaning inference of semantically transparent compounds more complex is the semantic relation between the head and modifier. For instance, *chocolate bar* refers to "a bar that is made of chocolate," whereas the compound that has the same endocentric structure, *chocolate factory*, does not refer to "a factory that is made of chocolate," but instead refers to "a factory that makes chocolate." Furthermore, the meanings of less established or novel compounds, such as *chocolate book*, can be ambiguous, referring to either "a book that is about chocolate" or "a book that is made of chocolate." Thus, understanding of the head structure is not always sufficient for inferring the meaning of compounds, because compound inference is also based on various types of semantic relationships between the modifier and head.

The semantic relation in compounds is explained by the competition among relations in nominals model (Gagné and Shoben, 1997), which suggests that readers select the semantic relation for a given compound based on the frequency of the relations applied to the other compounds that use the same modifier. For example, the modifier, *mountain*, is more commonly interpreted as the location relation, such as in *mountain vacation* or *mountain weather*. When native speakers encounter new compounds, they are expected to identify the most common relation based on their own experience. In L2, learners' L1 as well as their experience using L2 compounds influences their relation selection. Although L2 research in this topic is limited, in a descriptive study with Chinese L1 ESL students, Zhou and Murphy (2011) reported that the students inferred the meaning of *cheeseburger* as "burger made of cheese," where the correct relation was "burger has cheese," indicating a part-whole relationship.

5.3 Chapter Summary

This chapter introduced the connection between written language and spoken language. Written language maps onto spoken language in a way that is unique to each language. Accordingly, the skills required for recognizing words are specific to the writing system and orthography of the language students are learning to read. Word recognition involves multiple levels of cognitive processing, requiring readers to access a word's orthographic (letter/written scripts), phonological, and morphological information simultaneously in order to access the word's meaning. Word recognition is crucial in literacy development because accurate reading comprehension depends on accurate and automatic word recognition.

For L2 learners, any words that contain linguistic properties and structures that are different from their L1s may be subject to the influence of cross-linguistic transfer. Learners' sensitivity or insensitivity to any aspect of word-form information (phonological, orthographic, and morphological) can lead to the extraction of inaccurate information, and the inaccurately extracted word-form information may result in inaccurate word-meaning inference. Thus, it is important to develop word recognition skills for the accurate extraction of word-form information.

6

Generating Contextual Information

The Cognitive Model of Word-Meaning Inference asserts that learners make use of contextual information for inferring the meanings of unknown words encountered during reading. This chapter describes the underlying processes required for generating the contextual information: processing and interpretation of sentences and comprehension of messages from a text. The first section of the chapter summarizes the theories and models in sentence processing and interpretation, which clarifies how local contextual information is generated. The second section summarizes the theories and models in comprehension of larger portions of text, which clarifies how global contextual information is generated. The third section introduces the influence of cross-linguistic transfer in sentence processing and interpretation and reading comprehension, which can affect the quality of the contextual information to be used for word-meaning inference.

6.1 Theories and Models in Sentence Processing

6.1.1 Factors That Affect Sentence Processing and Interpretation

One of the factors that can influence sentence processing is the length and structural complexity of sentences. Generally speaking, sentences that are longer and have more complex structures are considered to be more difficult to interpret. Let us look at some examples here.

(1) I like apples.
(2) I like apples that the local farmers grow because they are fresher than the ones we can find at stores.
(3) I like *apples* [that the local farmers grow] [because they are fresher than the *ones* [we can find at stores]].

Sentence (1) has a simple structure with a subject (S)—verb (V)—object (O) order. We interpret (1) more easily than (2) because (2) has multiple subordinate clauses embedded within the main clause, "I like apples," as shown in (3). The clause, *that the local farmers grow*, modifies *apples*, and the clause that begins with *because . . .* is connected to the main clause with a coordinating conjunction, *because*. Within this clause, the subordinate clause, *we can find at stores*, modifies *ones*. It is also important to understand what the pronouns, *they* and *ones* refer to. Nevertheless, sentence length and structural complexity is not always a predictor of sentence interpretation difficulty because lengthy and complex sentences are often due to efforts to make the sentence semantically more coherent (e.g., Davison, Wilson, and Hermon, 1985). For example, Koda (2005) explains that readers have to interpret the semantic relationship between the two sentences in (4a), whereas in (4b) the relationship is clearly indicated by the word, *because*. In (4a), several different conjunctions could fit in the sentence, such as an indication of time frame (e.g., *before*, *after*) or contrast (e.g., *but*, *although*), which makes it more difficult for readers to understand the message from the two separate sentences.

(4a) We started the party. John arrived.
(4b) We started the party because John arrived.

Another factor is the role of syntactic knowledge in sentence interpretation. Crain and Shankweiler (1988) introduced two positions: the structural deficit hypothesis and the processing deficit hypothesis. The structural deficit hypothesis assumes that a lack of syntactic knowledge is the main cause of difficulty in sentence processing and interpretation. Syntactic knowledge develops according to a hierarchy of structural complexity, which explains why beginning-level learners have difficulty in sentence processing and interpretation. For example, (5a) and (5b) differ by only one word, *and* or *that*. Which sentence has a more complex structure?

(5a) The dog hit a cat and bit a rat.
(5b) The dog hit a cat that bit a rat.

(5b) has a more complex structure because the subordinate clause, or more specifically, the relative clause, *that bit a rat*, modifies the noun, *cat*. Because of the complexity, beginning level readers might have more difficulty interpreting (5b) than (5a). On the other hand, the processing deficit hypothesis assumes that syntactic development comes from innate ability. Children who are beginning to read in their L1s are prewired and considered to possess sufficient syntactic knowledge. Difficulty in sentence interpretation is due to issues in processing, mainly, a lack of fluency in word recognition, which can consume working memory capacity necessary for sentence interpretation. Let us experience how readers with limited word recognition skills might read (5a).

The

dog

hit

a

cat

and

bit

a

rat

If readers are struggling to recognize words in a sentence, then by the time they reach the last word in the sentence, they would probably have to reread the beginning part of the sentence. This is because they cannot maintain the lexical information of the words they recognize in their working memory for interpreting the meaning of the sentence.

6.1.2 What Is Syntactic Parsing?

When we read, we extract lexical information through word recognition processes, and the extracted lexical information is integrated according to the grammar of the target language. This integration process is called syntactic parsing. This section introduces the mechanisms of syntactic parsing, which can affect the kind of local contextual information L2 learners generate from interpreting a sentence during word-meaning inference from reading. To begin with, what message do you generate from the following sentence?

The cat chased the mouse.

In order to generate the message, we identify the parts of speech of the words and analyze the phrasal structures as follows:

[The cat] [chased [the mouse]].
   NP   NP VP

The cat is a subject noun phrase (NP), which is the doer of the action indicated by the main verb, *chased*. The predicate verb phrase (VP) is *chased the mouse*. Within the VP, there is also another NP, which indicates the object of the action, namely, the receiver of the action, *chased*. Inflectional morphemes also provide important information in sentence interpretation. In the example, the verb, *chase*, has a past tense morpheme, *-ed*, which signals that the action happened in the past. In syntactic parsing studies, researchers often use sentences that require more complex processing because those sentences can reveal how readers' minds work more clearly than sentences that do not require complex processing. Let us examine the following sentence:

(6)   The horse raced past the barn fell.

At first, you probably interpreted the sentence as in (6a). In this interpretation, the first NP, *The horse*, was identified as the subject, and *raced* was identified as the main verb.

(6a)   The horse raced past the barn.

When you continued reading the words in the sentence, you probably had to stop and rethink at this word:

fell?

You must have been confused with the verb, *fell*. This is due to the fact that *fell* did not fit in the grammar structure you were assuming in order to interpret the sentence. The verb, *fell*, did not belong to the phrasal structure of (6a).

What proficient readers do at this point is to try another interpretation by reanalyzing the sentence structure. The reanalyzed structure is (6b), in which the subject NP is *The horse raced past the barn*. The subject NP can be interpreted more clearly with the addition of a relative pronoun and auxiliary verb, *that was*, as indicated in brackets.

(6b) The horse [that was] raced past the barn fell.

In this reanalysis, *fell* is the main verb, which makes the interpretation successful and complete. The ambiguity in the sentence is due to the reduced relative clause (omission of *that was*). The omission misleads most readers to falsely identify *raced* as the main verb in the initial interpretation. This type of ambiguous sentence is also called a garden path sentence, because it misleads readers to the wrong interpretation at first. The next two sections introduce the major models in syntactic parsing to further explain the parsing processes: the garden path model and the constraint-based model.

6.1.3 Garden Path Model

The garden path model proposes that we parse sentences in a sequential manner, pursuing one interpretation at a time (Frazier, 1987). There are two principles that facilitate the parsing stages in this model. The first principle is minimum attachment. The parser integrates incoming information into the phrase in a way that makes the interpretation structurally simpler. Let us examine the principle using (6).

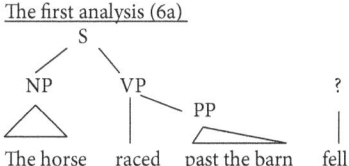

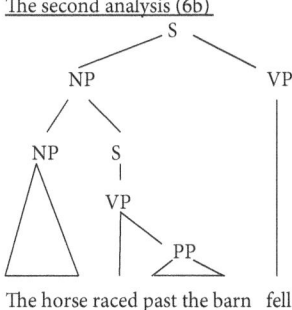

Figure 6.1 Example of the minimum attachment principle.

The first analysis in (6a) identifies *raced* as the main verb. When we reach the word, *fell*, we realize that this analysis does not work and conduct the second analysis, which leads to the correct interpretation. Figure 6.1 illustrates the syntactic structure of the first and second interpretations. Notice that the structure is simpler in the first analysis than in the second analysis. According to the minimum attachment principle, we choose the least complex structure at first, although the structure we select may not lead to the correct interpretation in ambiguous sentences such as (6).

The second principle of the garden path model is late closure, which states that we interpret sentences by attaching incoming information to the phrase or clause that is currently being processed. Let us examine the following sentence as an example.

(7) I convinced her children are noisy.

In sentence (7), at which word did you have to reanalyze the structure? It must have been the word, *are*, because most readers would interpret the sentence as follows in (7a).

(7a) I convinced her children.

   are?

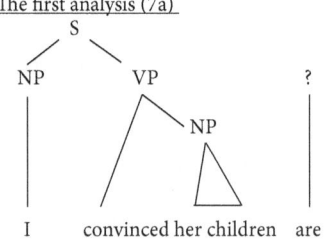

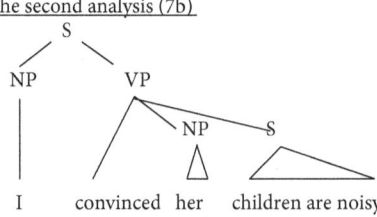

Figure 6.2 Example of the late closure principle.

In the first analysis in (7a), the misanalysis occurs because we attach *children* to the same phrase as *her*, structuring *her children* as an NP. The reanalyzed structure is shown in (7b). The omission of the complementizer, *that*, misleads us to the inaccurate interpretation in the first analysis. The syntactic structures of the two analyses of (7) are illustrated in Figure 6.2.

(7b) I convinced her [that] children are noisy.

6.1.4 Constraint-Based Models

Constraint-based models argue that factors other than syntactic structure (e.g., word meanings, frequency of the co-occurrence of words, and sentence discourse) also influence the way we interpret sentences (e.g., McDonald, Pearlmutter, and Seidenberg, 1994). For example, Crain and Steedman (1985) used a grammaticality judgment task to determine the influence of plausibility in sentence processing. In their study, adult readers judged the grammaticality of garden path sentences with reduced relative clauses, such as, *The teachers/ students taught by the educational method passed the exam.* Although both sentences were grammatical, the researchers found that their participants identified the sentence that started with *The students* as grammatical more easily than the sentence that started with *The teachers*. The difference was explained as due to the influence of plausibility (i.e., the frequency of co-occurrence between the two words: teacher-taught vs. students-taught) based on world knowledge. The participants were more easily garden pathed to the interpretation of *The teachers* as the doer (or agent) of "taught," which led them to make the judgment that the sentence beginning with *The teachers* did not make sense.

Focusing on the semantic characteristics of nouns, Ferreira and Clifton (1986) compared English L1 college students' eye movement while interpreting sentences such as the following, *The defendant/evidence examined by the prosecutor was reliable.* The prediction was that the students would be more likely to be garden pathed in the sentence that started with *The defendant* (an animate noun), than *The evidence* (an inanimate noun), which would not be able to take the action of *examine*. Against the prediction, the results indicated that they were garden pathed in both sentences, demonstrating that semantic information was not considered at the initial sentence parsing.

6.1.5 Anaphoric References and Comprehension

Understanding the references of pronouns is vital for accurate comprehension. Let us examine the following example: *Mary won and John lost. She was happy and he was sad*. In the example, we are able to identify that *she* refers to *Mary* and *he* refers to *John* by making use of gender knowledge. However, when interpreting sentences with more than one reference possibility, we need to take into account semantic factors in sentence parsing (e.g., Stewart, Pickering, and Sanford, 2000). For example, in (8a), the pronoun, *she*, refers to *Mary*, because we think if someone is being too loud, that is the person who should apologize. In contrast, in (8b), the pronoun, *she*, refers to *Sarah*, because we think if someone has been treated unfairly, that is the person who deserves an apology. In order to identify the antecedent of the pronoun, we need to understand the causal relationship between the first and the second clauses in the sentence.

(8a) Mary apologized to Sarah because she had been too loud.
(8b) Mary apologized to Sarah because she had been treated unfairly.

Our background knowledge is also important for identifying the antecedent of pronouns (Underwood and Batt, 1996). For example, in the sentence, *When the cat saw the mouse, it was terrified*, the knowledge that cats chase mice helps us understand that the pronoun, *it*, refers to the mouse. Depending on our background knowledge, we may choose an antecedent that is in fact ungrammatical. For example, for the sentence, "They had a feature on violent youngsters, attributing it to drink," Oakhill and Garnham (1992: 171) reported that their research participants thought the pronoun, *it*, referred to "violence" or "the violent behavior," which did not appear in the sentence. This example demonstrates that text comprehension involves readers' preexisting knowledge in addition to the words in the sentences.

6.1.6 Shallow Structure Hypothesis

One of the issues being debated in L2 sentence processing research is whether L2 learners are able to attain native-like sentence processing skills. Some learners seem to have adequate grammar knowledge but still have difficulty interpreting sentences accurately. Also, many learners take longer to interpret sentences than native speakers would. The shallow structure hypothesis (Clahsen and Felser, 2006; Felser and Roberts, 2007) maintains that adult L2 learners rely more on lexical, semantic, and pragmatic information to interpret sentences because they have difficulty achieving native-like syntactic processing skills.

For instance, Felser et al. (2003) examined whether German L1 and Greek L1 ESL students would identify the antecedent of a relative pronoun, *who*, differently depending on the type of preposition (*with* or *of*) included in the noun phrase in which antecedent candidates were located. For example, in sentences, such as *We knew the professor with the student who was reading a book* and *We knew the student of the professor who was reading a book*, the students were asked to indicate who was reading the book. There were two possible interpretations, *the student* or *the professor*, in both of the sentences. The preposition, *of*, indicates the meaning of functional or occupational characteristics, whereas the preposition, *with*, indicates the meaning of accompaniment or attributive characteristics. The results indicated that the German L1 and Greek L1 ESL learners preferred the second NP (*the student*) as the antecedent in the sentence with the preposition, *with*, but showed no preference in the sentence with the preposition, *of*, whereas native speakers of English preferred the second NP for both prepositions. These findings demonstrated that the L2 learners depended less on syntactic structures but more on lexical-semantic information in interpreting the sentences.

6.1.7 Automaticity and Processing Capacity in L2 Sentence Processing

Nevertheless, a number of studies have demonstrated that L2 learners are capable of syntactically driven sentence processing, rejecting the shallow structure hypothesis (e.g., Dekydtspotter et al., 2012; Witzel, Witzel, and Nicol, 2012). Some studies further suggest that the difference between native speakers and L2 learners is due to a difference in resource allocation (e.g., Kaan, Ballantyne, and Wijnen, 2015; Lim and Christianson, 2013). Assuming that L2 learners have sufficient syntactic knowledge for sentence interpretation, their difficulty seems to be efficiency in integrating information generated through syntactic processing for comprehension, rather than in syntactic processing itself. Automaticity is defined as fast and effortless processing and is essential in L2 development (Segalowitz, 2003). In sentence processing, readers need to be able to integrate different sources of linguistic information (lexical/semantic, morphological, syntactic, and pragmatic knowledge) simultaneously. Unautomatized processing in any one of the information sources can cause a slow down or a break down in sentence processing.

Cunnings (2017) provides further explanation of where the difficulty in L2 sentence processing comes from. The non-nativeness in L2 sentence processing is considered to be caused by the inability to retrieve information constructed during sentence processing from working memory. For example, the sentence, *This is the book I recommend*, includes a relative clause, which combines two sentences into one.

This is the book + I recommend the book.
→ This is the book (that) I recommend [ ].

When the two sentences are combined, the second sentence is attached to the first sentence with the relative pronoun, *that*, which can be omitted. When the sentences are combined, *the book* at the end of the second sentence needs to be dropped, which leaves an empty slot at the end. In order to interpret the sentence accurately, readers need to retrieve the information that *the book* is the object of the verb, *recommend*, from their working memory during sentence processing. According to Cunnings (2017), L2 learners are more susceptible to interference during this retrieval process, leading to inaccurate or slower interpretation.

6.1.8 Development of L2 Syntactic Processing

Some findings suggest that L2 learners who are at an advanced level of proficiency are able to perform sentence interpretation tasks in a native-like manner (e.g., Conroy and Cupples, 2010; Coughlin and Tremblay, 2013; Omaki and Schultz, 2011). Conroy and Cupples (2010) found that ESL students with advanced proficiency showed the same patterns of sentence processing as native speakers in sentences that involved a more complex structure. For example, the sentence, *He could have painted the room*, has the modal perfect structure (*could have painted*), which indicates the meaning of counterfactual action, whereas in the sentence, *He could have paint in the room*, the verb, *have*, is a lexical verb that indicates the meaning of possession.

The researchers hypothesized that the native speakers would be better (faster and more accurate) at processing sentences with the modal perfect structure exhibiting the preference for late closure, whereas the ESL students would not show any difference between the two structures. Against the prediction, the results indicated that both the ESL learners and native speakers were better at processing the sentences with the modal perfect structure, suggesting that the L2 learners could achieve the same level of syntactic sensitivity as native speakers.

The interface hypothesis (Sorace, 2011; Sorace and Filiaci, 2006) acknowledges the developmental differences in L2 sentence processing. Interface is defined as "syntactic structures that are sensitive to conditions of varying nature (Sorace, 2011: 6)." The hypothesis states that language structures involving an interface between syntax and other cognitive domains are more difficult to acquire than structures that do not involve such an interface. For example, Sorace and Filiaci (2006) investigated how near-native speakers of Italian L2 would identify the antecedent of overt pronouns (explicitly stated pronouns). In the study, the near-native and native speakers identified the antecedent in two types of sentences: a sentence in which the pronoun followed the antecedent (forward anaphora), such as, the Italian equivalent of *The mother talks to her sister, while she is reading the letter*, and a sentence in which the pronoun preceded the antecedent (backward anaphora), such as, the Italian equivalent of *While she is reading the letter, the mother talks to her sister*.

The researchers found that both the natives and near natives preferred the complement (*her sister*) as the antecedent for the overt pronoun (*she*) in the sentence with forward anaphora. However, in the sentence with backward anaphora, the near natives preferred the subject (*the mother*) as the antecedent, while the natives preferred an extralinguistic referent (someone not mentioned in the sentence) as the antecedent. The findings demonstrated that some syntactic structures require more advanced knowledge and experience in the L2.

6.2 Theories and Models in Reading Comprehension

6.2.1 What it Means to Comprehend a Text

Have you ever felt this before?—"I understand what is written but I don't quite understand what it means." This is how most of us would feel if we did not have a deeper level of reading comprehension. Being able to interpret each sentence written in a text does not necessarily mean that we are able to obtain deeper comprehension of the text. Depending on our prior experience and knowledge, some of us may not have deeper comprehension of a text on a specialized topic, such as medicine, law, auto mechanics, video games, pets, etc. Deeper comprehension involves processes beyond what is written in a text. When we process the text beyond what is written, we create a mental representation of the text based on both the textual information and our preexisting knowledge (Johnson-Laird, 1983; van Dijk and Kintsch, 1983).

A mental representation can be described as being similar to creating a visual image of the text in the reader's head. Let us examine the following sentences.

A butterfly sat on a lily pad. A tadpole swam under the lily pad.

After reading the sentences, most of us would create a mental representation similar to Figure 6.3.

If anyone asks us where the butterfly was, we would be able to say it was above the tadpole based on the image, even though the information being asked for is not stated anywhere. When we understand information that is not explicitly stated in the text, we are making inferences. Note that "inference" discussed here refers to an inference from a text, which differs from "inference" in word-meaning inference. By making inferences, we are able to create a mental representation of the text for deeper comprehension. For the example given earlier, we are able to make inferences because of our knowledge about logical relationships: if A is above B, and C is under B, then A is above C.

A deeper level of comprehension also necessitates more specific knowledge to fill in the information not explicitly stated. For example, in the sentence, *Mothers' Day is coming up next week. John decided to go shopping at the mall*, readers would need to fill in the information that the purpose of the shopping

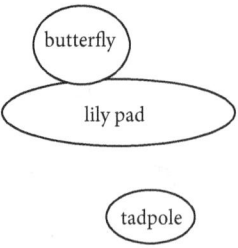

Figure 6.3 Mental representation of the butterfly, lily pad, and tadpole

trip is to buy a present for his mother, based on cultural knowledge about Mothers' Day and gift giving.

How do L2 learners make inferences and achieve deeper comprehension? This is an important question because the level of comprehension directly affects the quality of contextual information the learners generate for word-meaning inference. Some research suggests that the mental representation created by reading in L1 is different from the representation created by reading in L2. For example, Jenkin et al. (1993) reported that college-level French L1 ESL learners and English L1 learners of French demonstrated different mental images for a set of sentences, such as the example shown later. The students responded differently to a diagram of the objects' spatial arrangement depending on whether they read the sentences in L1 or L2.

The laptop is to the right of the book.
The printer is behind the book.

PRINTER
BOOK   LAPTOP

Furthermore, Horiba (1996) pointed out that L1 reading differs from L2 reading in terms of which process readers devote more of their cognitive attention to. In her study, English L1 college students read a text written in Japanese (L2) and in English. The results demonstrated that the students directed their attention more toward higher-level comprehension processes in L1 reading and more toward lower-level processes in L2 reading.

6.2.2 Schema Theory

The schema theory maintains that our background knowledge determines what we comprehend from a text (Anderson and Pearson, 1984). A schema is preexisting knowledge about stereotypical situations stored in long-term memory. For example, a restaurant schema may include what we normally do when we arrive at a restaurant, such as wait to be seated, sit at a table, order a drink, order a meal, etc. In order to achieve a deeper level of reading comprehension, we need to fill the information obtained from the text into our preexisting schema. Lack of an appropriate schema or inability to identify an appropriate schema results in comprehension breakdown. Let us read the following example. What do you think this passage describes?

> It is one of the things that almost everyone has experienced in their life. It is not the sort of thing that they enjoy, and in fact, most people dislike it. However, they still do it if it's necessary. There are various forms it can take, although it seems there are a few that are most common.

For example, in Bransford and Johnson (1972), English L1 high school students read a passage that was written in a way that was so general that it was difficult to activate any schema. The results indicated that the students who were given the topic of the passage before reading scored higher on comprehension (self-rated) and recall (writing down essential ideas from the passage) than the students who were not given the topic or received the topic after reading. They concluded that the availability of the topic before reading helped the students establish the appropriate schema, which was "washing clothes."

Similarity, McKoon and Ratcliff (1981) maintained that the first step of reading comprehension is to access preexisting knowledge in memory. In their study, English L1 participants read a short passage that would activate an instrumental inference. After reading the passage, the participants were shown a target word and responded whether the word appeared in the passage. The participants responded more quickly to the word (*hammer*) when the final sentence of the passage included the words, "pounded the boards together with nails," rather than the words, "stuck the boards together with glue." The difference was explained as due to the schemata associated with the verbs, *pound* and *stuck*. The verb, *pound*, activated the schema that included instruments necessary for pounding (e.g., a hammer). The findings demonstrated that schemata could also affect the memory and recall of a text.

6.2.3 Construction-Integration Model

The construction-integration model (Kintsch, 1988, 1998) maintains that reading comprehension is a result of information processing, which encompasses two processes: construction and integration. In the construction process, readers construct a textbase, which is the proposition (or message) generated from understanding of words and phrases in a text. The propositions are connected to create the microstructure (localized understanding of the text), which is further connected to create the macrostructure (global understanding of the text). These structures are integrated into a larger discourse context.

Propositions are structured in a way that they are connected to each other. When a new proposition is introduced, readers need to keep the information from the new proposition in working (or short-term) memory until it is structured appropriately and stored in long-term memory. The construction-integration model considers efficient word recognition to be a critical factor, because readers who are fast and accurate in word recognition can establish a textbase for subsequent comprehension more efficiently, leaving more cognitive capacity for the integration process.

For a deeper level of comprehension, readers also create situation models (van Dijk and Kintsch, 1983), which are mental representations more specific to individual instances in a text, rather than relatively fixed preexisting knowledge as in schemata. Situation models are known to be multi-dimensional, including representations of special locations, time sequence, causal relationships, and the goals and motives of the characters in the story (Zwaan, 1999). For example, when readers create a representation of the distance between two entities, the distance between an elephant and a river is expected to be larger than the distance between an ant and a river. For another example, readers predict the action of a story based on causal relationship, so that if a character was "standing the whole time," then the character should be tired and want to sit down.

6.2.4 Top-Down, Bottom-Up, and Interactive Approaches

Reading models are generally categorized into top-down, bottom-up, or interactive approaches. The categorization is not for describing the model itself, but rather for illustrating the theoretical approaches taken by each model. Grabe (2009) also states that the three terms are based on a metaphorical notion of how the model works. Top-down approaches of reading comprehension emphasize a reader's own views more than individual words in a text, as shown in the schema theory (Anderson and Pearson, 1984). Under this approach, reading is viewed as a psycholinguistic guessing game. It is considered that readers hypothesize the message from the text by making use of their preexisting background knowledge (Goodman, 1967, 1970).

They may identify some cues in the text, such as the title of the book, key words, or pictures, and make use of them to activate background knowledge, but it is assumed that fluent readers do not need to pay attention to each individual word.

Bottom-up approaches of reading comprehension emphasize the importance of lower-level processes (see more in Chapter 4). Orthographic, phonological, morphological, and semantic processing leads to the processing of letters and words, necessary for the processing of phrases and sentences, which in turn leads to the processing of paragraphs and text at the discourse level, as introduced in the construction-integration model (Kintsch, 1988, 1998). Some of the evidence supporting bottom-up approaches comes from eye movement research, demonstrating that fluent readers do look at almost all of the words in a text (Carpenter and Just, 1983; Just and Carpenter, 1980). The bottom-up approaches stress the importance of word recognition in reading comprehension (see more in Chapter 5).

Interactive approaches incorporate the premises from both the top-down and bottom-up approaches, assuming that both processes occur more or less simultaneously and influence each other. There is support from both L1 and L2 research (e.g., Carrell, Devine, and Eskey, 1988; Coady, 1993; Lesgold and Perfetti, 1981), although exactly how the interactive processing occurs seems to remain unspecified. Grabe (2009) points out that it would be less likely to have higher-level processing in comprehension (i.e., inference) impact word recognition in lower-level processing, because word recognition is supposed to be automatized and therefore free from intentional control.

6.3 Cross-Linguistic Transfer during the Generation of Contextual Information

6.3.1 Cross-linguistic Variation in Sentence Processing

The garden path model explains sentence parsing principles in English, yet the same principles are not always operative in languages other than English. Research has reported that the late closure principle does not apply to native speakers of Spanish (e.g., Cuetos and Mitchell, 1988), French (e.g., Zagar, Pynte, and Rativeau, 1997), and Dutch (Brysbaert and Mitchell, 1996). One of the sentence structures examined in the studies was relative clauses, such as, *The counselor assisted the teacher of the student who had become ill*. In interpreting the sentence, who do you think is the agent (or subject) of the relative clause, "had become ill"? There are two possibilities, either *the teacher* or *the student*. Using similar sentences, Cuetos and Mitchell (1988) investigated whether the choice of the agent would differ between native speakers of English and native speakers of Spanish. The results indicated that the native speakers of English preferred the second noun phrase, *the student* in the example, following the late closure principle. In contrast, the native speakers of Spanish preferred the first noun phrase, *the teacher* in the example, demonstrating a preference for early closure.

The head structure of a language is another factor in cross-linguistic variation in sentence processing (Mazuka and Itoh, 1995). English is a head-initial language, whereas Japanese is a head-final language. The head verb is in the initial position of the phrase in English, whereas it is in the phrase final position in Japanese, as shown in the examples of VPs given here.

go to the library
toshyokan   ni   iku
"the library" "to" "go"

This is the negation of the example.

did not go to the library
toshyokan   ni   ika   na   katta
"the library" "to" "go" "not" past

As shown in the aforementioned example, in Japanese, some of the critical information, such as the information about negation or tense, is presented at the end of the phrase, which requires readers to wait to make an interpretation until the final word in the phrase. Consequently, interpretation decisions are delayed until the head is reached, compared to English.

Fender (2003) investigated whether there would be cross-linguistic differences in L2 sentence processing between Arabic L1 and Japanese L1 college-level ESL students. In the study, the students performed a lexical decision task and a sentence reading task. The results indicated that the

Japanese L1 ESL students were faster and more accurate in the lexical decision task, which was attributed to their higher sensitivity to English orthography as reported in a number of ESL word recognition studies (e.g., Akamatsu, 1999; Brown and Haynes, 1985). In contrast, the Arabic L1 ESL students were more accurate in the sentence reading task, which was attributed to the typological similarity between Arabic and English phrasal and clausal structures.

6.3.2 How Do Learners Identify the Agent of a Sentence?

The competition model (Bates and MacWhinney, 1989) contends that sentence interpretation is a result of the competition between various cues, such as word order, case marking (e.g., *they* is nominal case, but *them* is accusative case), animacy status of a word, and agreement (e.g., *the cat chase* vs. *the cat chases*). The cue strength varies across languages, and the competition model suggests that cue strength in L1 can transfer to L2 sentence processing. For example, word order is not the strongest cue in Spanish, due to the fact that word order is more flexible in Spanish, allowing SOV, VSO, and OVS orders. For instance, in the following example, what is the agent (doer) of the action?

   the cat   chases   the mouse
     S   V   O

The example has an SVO word order. The noun for the subject NP, *cat*, is animate and able to execute the action of *chase*. However, the following example poses a question.

   the book chases the mouse

Although the sentence is in the SVO word order and grammatical, the noun in the subject NP, *book*, is inanimate, which cannot execute the action of *chase*. According to the competition model, English readers tend to depend more on the word-order cue. Consequently, it can be predicted that they would likely to consider *book* as the agent because that is the first NP (left most) in the sentence. Let us examine the following examples.

   (9)   the cats chases the mouse
   (10) them chase the mouse

The examples both have an SVO word order. However, in (9), the agreement between *cats* (plural) and *chases* (singular) is violated, and in (10), the case marking for the noun in the subject NP position (the first NP from the left), *them*, is violated. In both examples, it is predicted that English readers would be likely to interpret the first NP as the agent, *the cats* in (9) and *them* (interpreted as *they*) in (10).

A number of studies have reported that L1 cue preference transfers to L2 sentence processing, comparing English and another language, such as Chinese (e.g., Su, 2001, 2004), German (e.g., Kilborn, 1989), Japanese (e.g., Sasaki, 1991; Yoshimura and MacWhinney, 2010), and Spanish (e.g., Morett and MacWhinney, 2013). For example, Kilborn (1989) compared sentence interpretation between German L1 ESL learners and native speakers of English, using sentences with various word orders, such as shown in the examples.

(11) N V N (the chair moves the mother)
(12) V N N (cooks the chair the book)
(13) N N V (the chairs the mother moves)

In (11), the animacy cue is being tested because the noun in the subject NP position, *the chair*, is inanimate. In (12), the animacy and word-order cues are being tested because both Ns are inanimate. In (13), the word-order and agreement cues are being tested, because the noun in the subject NP position, *chairs* (plural) does not agree with the verb, *moves* (singular).

In the Kilborn study, the task was to indicate the subject (agent) of the sentence. When the task was administered in English, the results indicated that native speakers of English relied heavily on the word-order cue, while the German L1 learners of English L2 relied more on the agreement and animacy cues. Importantly, the English L2 learners' cue preference was identical to when they performed the same task in their L1 using the German equivalent of the sentences. The results demonstrated that the learners' L1 cue preferences transferred to L2 sentence processing. These findings imply that how L2 learners identify the agent of a sentence may affect the generation of local contextual information.

6.3.3 Sensitivity to Agreement

Grammatical morphemes are often challenging to L2 learners. For example, Jiang (2004, 2007) investigated sensitivity to plural morphemes, using sentences such as, *The questions to the teacher are due this coming Friday* and *The question to the teacher are due this coming Friday*. The second example is ungrammatical because *question* (singular), does not agree with the verb, *are*. In Jiang (2004), native speakers of English and Chinese L1 ESL learners read a series of sentences such as the examples above, and their sentence comprehension and reading speed were compared. The results demonstrated that native speakers of English took longer to read the ungrammatical sentences, demonstrating sentence processing breakdown, whereas Chinese L1 ESL learners did not show any differences between the grammatical and ungrammatical sentences, presumably, due to "the fact that grammatical number is seldom encoded in their L1, Chinese" (Jiang, 2004: 627).

Similarly, Kaan, Ballantyne, and Wijnen (2015) demonstrated that Dutch ESL students experienced difficulty in identifying the subject-verb agreement in relative clause sentences. In English, in the subject relative clause, the verb for the relative pronoun agrees with the NP located outside of the relative clause, such as, *The counselor knows the coach who was fair to the students*. In the object relative clause, the verb for the relative pronoun agrees with the NP located within the relative clause, such as *The counselor knows the coach who the students were talking about*. However, in Dutch, for both subject and object relative clauses, the verb follows the two NPs, and the antecedent of the relative pronoun is indicated by an agreement marker. In the study, the researchers found that the ESL students falsely judged sentences such as, *The counselor knows the coach who the students has been complaining about*, as grammatical because it was acceptable in their L1.

6.3.4 Structural Difference in Verb Usage

There are some verbs that share similar meanings between different languages, yet the structural requirements for the verbs are not necessarily identical. Studies have suggested that structural difference in verb usage affects L2 sentence interpretation (e.g., Frenck-Mestre and Pynte, 1997; Inagaki, 2001, 2002; Montrul, 2001). For example, Inagaki (2001) examined the structural difference of manner-of-motion verbs (e.g., *walk*, *run*) and directed motion verbs (e.g., *go*) between English and Japanese. In English, both types of verbs can be used with a prepositional phrase (PP), expressing the goal, such as, *Mary walked to the store* and *Mary went to the store*. However, Japanese allows only directed motion verbs to occur with a goal PP. Therefore, in Japanese, the direct translation of *Mary walked to the store* is ungrammatical, whereas *Mary went to the store* is grammatical. In the study, the researcher found that Japanese L1 ESL learners were able to correctly judge English sentences with a manner-of-motion verb and a goal PP as grammatical, while English L1 Japanese L2 learners were not able to judge the Japanese translation of *Mary walked to the store* as ungrammatical.

Likewise, Montrul (2001) compared the difference in manner-of-motion verbs between English and Spanish. In English, a manner-of-motion verb, such as *march*, can be used in a sentence with a direct object if it is accompanied by a PP, such as, *The teacher marched the students to the classroom*, whereas in Spanish, it is ungrammatical to add a direct object even if it is accompanied by a PP. In the study, the accuracy of the grammaticality judgment was compared between two groups of Spanish L2 learners, learners with English L1 and Turkish L1. The hypothesis was that the Turkish L1 learners of Spanish would outperform the English L1 learners of Spanish, due to the structural similarity between Turkish and Spanish. The results indicated that the Turkish L1 group was more accurate in identifying the sentences with a PP as ungrammatical than the English L1 group, demonstrating L1 transfer in L2 sentence processing.

6.3.5 How Do L2 Readers Interpret Pronouns?

Sentences that include pronouns can be difficult to process in L2. In a pro-drop language, such as Spanish, it is possible to omit a pronoun in the second clause. Jegerski, van Pattern, and Keating (2011) examined whether Spanish L2 learners would be able to identify the antecedent of a null pronoun (omitted pronoun) in a native-like manner in sentences such as *Mary always emailed Sarah when (she) was in the US*. The null pronoun typically refers to the NP in the subject position (*Mary* in the example), while the overt pronoun (*she* in the example) refers to the NP in the object position (*Sarah* in the example). In the study, both intermediate and advanced proficiency English L1 learners of Spanish L2 failed to show native-like differentiation in identifying the antecedent between the null and overt pronouns in Spanish.

Another type of pronoun that can be problematic in L2 sentence processing is relative pronouns. For instance, Juffs (1998) examined whether L2 learners would have difficulty interpreting the following type of garden path sentence with a reduced relative clause, such as, *The dog watched all the time was running around*. In the example, the correct interpretation requires filling in the reduced relative pronoun and auxiliary verb after *dog*, as follows: *The dog [that was] watched* . . . The misinterpretation to assume *watched* as the main verb, as in *The dog watched* . . ., was predicted to cause a breakdown in interpreting the sentence. The participants were three typologically grouped ESL learners: Romance language L1 (Spanish, Italian, French, and Portuguese), Chinese L1, and Japanese and Korean L1. The patterns of reading speed indicated that the Romance L1 ESL learners performed most similarly to native speakers of English, which was attributed to the similarity in relative clause structure between the Romance languages and English.

Likewise, Witzel, Witzel, and Nicol (2012) investigated the interpretation of sentences that included relative pronouns such as, *The wife of the man who defended herself from the accusation was on the news show* and *The wife of the man who defended himself from the accusation was on the news show*. In the examples, the reflexive pronouns (*herself* and *himself*) specified the antecedent of the relative pronoun, *who*. The first example was referred to as high attachment, because the antecedent was more distant from the relative pronoun than in the second example, which was referred to as low attachment due to the closer distance to the relative pronoun. The researchers found that native speakers of English were faster in interpreting the low attachment sentences, while Chinese L1 ESL students showed the opposite pattern.

6.3.6 Topic Familiarity

Carrell and her colleagues applied the schema theory to L2 reading instruction (e.g., Carrell, 1984b; Carrell and Eisterhold, 1988), stressing the importance of background knowledge in reading comprehension. As a result, a preview activity that aims to build background knowledge has become an integral part of L2 reading instruction (e.g., Echevarria, Vogt, and Short, 2013). If a text requires specific knowledge, such as historical events (cultural knowledge) or auto mechanics (specialized knowledge), it would be difficult for L2 learners without such knowledge to have a deeper level of comprehension, which in turn would affect the kind of global contextual information they generate during word-meaning inference.

A number of L2 studies have shown empirical support for the schema theory, most of which comes from findings on the role of background knowledge in reading comprehension accuracy (e.g., Alptekin, 2006; Bensoussan, 1998; Brantmeier, 2005; Carrell, 1984a; Horiba and Fukaya, 2015; Lee, 2009; Leeser, 2007; McNeil, 2011). For example, Bensoussan (1998) asked college-level Arabic and Hebrew L1 ESL learners to read a text on the topic of love and marriage. The results indicated that 23 percent of the wrong answers to the comprehension questions were driven by activation of false schemata (preexisting knowledge/opinion about the topic).

In the same vein, Alptekin (2006) investigated the impact of the schema theory in reading comprehension, using the nativization technique. Turkish L1 college-level EFL students read a story that was set in New York City in the early 1900s. One group read the original and the other group read a nativized version, in which some of the culturally specific words were replaced with culturally more familiar words (e.g., *Istanbul* for *New York City*, *mosque* for *church*). The reading comprehension data indicated that the nativized-text group outperformed the original-text group in inferential comprehension, although there was no difference in literal comprehension.

6.3.7 Cross-Linguistic Variation in Discourse Structure

Kaplan (1966, 1988) proposed the notion of contrastive rhetoric, suggesting that the way in which we formulate sentences and paragraphs varies across cultures and languages. The assumption behind this theory is that our thought patterns are reflected in discourse structure in both oral and written language. For example, English readers tend to have thought patterns that are linear in development, in which a topic statement is developed into a central argument through a series of supporting examples. In contrast, Arabic readers tend to expect paragraph development to be based on a series of parallel constructions including both positive and negative arguments.

Although Kaplan's theory is clearly not applicable to all instances of written and oral discourse, it highlights the need for the consideration of discourse structure in L2 reading comprehension. Although the number of findings seems to be limited, there are some studies that demonstrated the transfer of L1 discourse structure to L2 reading comprehension (Carrell, 1984c, Sharp, 2002). For instance, Carrell (1984c) asked four groups of college-level ESL learners (Spanish L1, Arabic L1, Korean and Chinese L1, and Malaysian L1) to read the following types of expository texts: comparison, problem/solution, causation, and collection of descriptions. The results on the text recall indicated that the groups demonstrated strength and weakness in different types of texts. For instance, the Spanish L1 learners had difficulty with the collection of descriptions type, while the Arabic L1 learners had difficulty with the causation type. Nevertheless, the cross-linguistic difference found in the Carrell study was not confirmed in a replication study by Tian (1990), with learners of English at a secondary school and college in Singapore.

6.3.8 Metacognitive Strategies

L2 learning strategies can be categorized into metacognitive, cognitive, and socioaffective strategies (e.g., Chamot and O'Malley, 1994; O'Malley et al., 1985). Metacognitive strategy refers to strategies that involve executive control of cognition, such as planning, monitoring, and evaluation of their own learning processes. Cognitive strategy refers to more specific learning tasks, such as note taking and grouping. Socioaffective strategy refers to communication strategies, such as cooperation and questioning for clarification.

The studies on reading comprehension seem to indicate possible cross-linguistic variation in the preference for different types of metacognitive strategies. For instance, Mokhtari and Reichard (2004) administered a survey, called the metacognitive awareness of reading strategies inventory (MARSI), to college-level EFL learners in Morocco and native speakers of English in the United States. The inventory was based on their earlier study developed for native-speaking Grade 6–12 children (Mokhtari and Reichard, 2002), which included three categories: global reading strategies (e.g., predicting what the text is about), problem-solving strategies (e.g., re-reading for better comprehension), and support reading strategies (e.g., using a dictionary). Overall, the two groups preferred to use similar types of strategies, yet the researchers found some dissimilarities. For instance, the US students preferred to use visual features (e.g., text features such as tables) more often than the Moroccan students did, which was attributed to the difference in text style between US and Moroccan culture. Moreover, using the MARSI, Alhaqbani and Riazi (2012) found that Arabic L2 learners with an African L1 background preferred to use global strategies more frequently than learners with an Asian L1 background did. Similarly, comparing two groups of EFL learners at a high school, Persian-Turkish bilinguals and Persian monolinguals, Afsharrad and Sadeghi Benis (2017) found that the bilingual learners used metacognitive strategies more often than their monolingual counterparts.

6.4 Chapter Summary

In word-meaning inference, contextual information for unknown words is generated through comprehending a text, both at the local level from the context immediately surrounding the unknown words and at the global level from a larger portion of the text. Learners need to be able to determine which words within a sentence should be parsed into phrases and chunks in order to comprehend the sentence. Learners also need to integrate the meanings they comprehend from the sentences into larger units at the discourse level, such as paragraphs and chapters, applying their knowledge of the topic as well as knowledge of discourse structures.

In L2 reading, cross-linguistic transfer can affect the ways in which learners parse sentences and integrate the meanings from sentences into larger units, which can in turn affect the quality of contextual information they generate for word-meaning inference. At present, the exact nature of the contextual information that learners generate in order to accurately infer the meanings of unknown words needs further clarification, although there are some studies on this topic, as introduced in Chapters 3 and 7. Further research is warranted for a fuller understanding of what contextual information entails in word-meaning inference.

7

Pedagogical Applications

The Cognitive Model of Word-Meaning Inference postulates that two types of information, word-form information and contextual information, contribute to word-meaning inference from reading. The extraction of word-form information from unknown words is carried out through word recognition processes, and the generation of contextual information is dependent on the quality of reading comprehension, as described in Chapters 5 and 6, respectively. The first section of this chapter introduces tasks that promote word recognition skills, which are important for the extraction of word-form information. The tasks include those that promote metalinguistic awareness (orthographic, phonological, and morphological awareness), as well as word recognition fluency. The second section of the chapter introduces tasks and approaches that are designed to promote sentence processing and reading comprehension, including metacognitive strategies, which are expected to facilitate the generation of local and global contextual information. The final section of the chapter introduces word-meaning inference instruction, summarizing the procedures and steps in word-meaning inference that have been shown to be effective, and offers recommendations for implementing word-meaning inference instruction.

7.1 Building Word Recognition Skills

7.1.1 Promoting Metalinguistic Awareness

Metalinguistic awareness is defined as awareness of "the abstract structure that organizes sets of linguistic rules without being directly instantiated in any of them" (Bialystok, 2001: 123). Among the aspects of metalinguistic awareness, awareness of the phonological, orthographic, and morphological properties of words is vital to the development of word recognition skills (see Koda, 2005). This section introduces some of the metalinguistic tasks that are commonly used in literacy research. These tasks ask students to pay attention to a specific property of a word and demonstrate their awareness by identifying or manipulating the property. Because the tasks are intended to promote metalinguistic awareness, they should be incorporated into lessons as word-focused exercises for beginning-level students on a regular basis. Teachers need to keep in mind that cross-linguistic transfer can influence students' performance when they encounter any words with phonological, orthographic, and morphological structures different from their L1.

7.1.1.1 *Phonological Awareness*

Phonological awareness tasks are typically oral tasks that ask students to pay attention to specific phonemes (e.g., Byrne and Fielding-Barnsley, 1995; Goswami and Bryant, 1990). These tasks are particularly important for beginning-level students, including those who have not yet started reading written words. The tasks can be categorized as either phonological segmentation (identifying phonemes) or phonological blending (combining phonemes) (Torgesen, Morgan, and Davis, 1992), as shown in the samples below. The tasks are also expected to help the students make connections between phonemes and graphemes when they start reading written words.

> If you delete the first sound of the word, what word will you have? – *hear* (Answer: *ear*)
> Which word does not have the same sound at the beginning? – *cat, farm, kid* (Answer: *farm*)
> Which word has the same first sound as the word, *cat*? – *farm, kid* (Answer: *kid*)
> What word is this? – (Pronounce each phoneme) /k/ /æ/ /t/. (Answer: *cat*)

7.1.1.2 *Orthographic Awareness*

A spelling task is one of the most commonly used tasks for measuring orthographic awareness. In the spelling task, teachers may include words with both regular (e.g., *book, take, tail*) and irregular (e.g., *iron, shoe, gauge*) grapheme-phoneme correspondences and explain that some words are not spelled the way they are pronounced. When asking students to spell a word, it is important to give them a context. For example, Holmes and Carruthers (1998) asked English L1 college students to first listen to sentences that included target words and then write down the words. The target words were characterized as orthographically difficult, containing irregular grapheme-phoneme correspondences, such as *jeopardy* and *bureaucracy* (e.g., The demonstrators are demanding a change in the bureaucracy). In order to spell these words, the students needed to rely on their word-specific orthographic knowledge.

In a spelling task, the items to be spelled can be either real words or pseudowords. For pseudowords, students have to use their phonological and orthographic awareness, because they cannot rely on their existing vocabulary knowledge. For example, in a study by Mimeau, Ricketts, and Deacon (2018), teachers pronounced pseudowords, such as *veap*, *seef*, and *merl*, and asked children to spell them. Similarly, Deacon (2012) asked students to choose a correct spelling from phonologically plausible options, including the correct answer and a pseudo-homophone (e.g., choose *feed* or *fead*. Answer: *feed*), based on the items used by Olson, Forsberg, and Wise (1994). Measuring both orthographic and phonological awareness, Nassaji (2003b) asked college-level ESL students to work on two tasks, based on the items used by Manis et al. (1990), as shown in the samples provided below. In the phonological awareness task, the students were asked to determine whether a pair of pseudowords sounded the same or different. In the orthographic awareness task, the students compared the letter sequences of a pair of pseudowords and indicated the one that could be a real English word.

Which one looks more like an English word? – *fint*, *tinf* (Answer: *fint*)
Do these sound the same or different? – *cerb*, *serb* (Answer: same)

7.1.1.3 *Programmatic Approaches*

Phonics is probably one of the most prominent programs designed to develop native-speaking children's phonological and orthographic awareness, and it also has been recommended for ESL/EFL students (August and Shanahan, 2006; Reed, 2013). Effective phonics should be implemented in a meaningful and contextualized manner, although phonics is often misunderstood as simply the teaching of phonological rules. Stahl (1992) argues that phonics should focus on reading words, not learning rules, and provides several recommendations. Teachers should explain the rules of grapheme-phoneme correspondences while integrating the rules into reading comprehension of stories. In addition, teachers should focus on developing students' word recognition strategies, while clarifying the internal structure of words, including onsets and rhymes, as well as developing students' word recognition fluency (automaticity), so that they can devote their attention more to reading comprehension.

Phonics has been implemented as a literacy program in a number of schools. For example, in a study with Grade 1 students (age five) in New Zealand, Carson, Gillon, and Boustead (2013) implemented a 10-week program that directed the students' attention to making explicit connections between spoken words and printed words. Each week, the students received four thirty-minute phonological awareness lessons, including a review of the previous lesson (five minutes), phonological awareness activities, using various games, such as bingo (twenty minutes), and shared reading using a book, with emphasis on the phonological awareness skill targeted for that week (five minutes). The targeted phonological skills included phoneme identification, blending, segmentation, and manipulation (creating new words by changing phonemes). The researchers found that the students in the program improved their word reading and spelling scores significantly more than their counterparts who participated in a traditional literacy program.

Applying the lexical quality hypothesis (Perfetti, 2007; Perfetti and Hart, 2002) (see Chapter 4) to an instructional setting, Kucan (2012) suggests that vocabulary instruction should encompass all aspects of linguistic knowledge. For example, for building orthographic and phonological knowledge, teachers can display words in written form on a poster or word cards and have students pronounce them. For building semantic knowledge, teachers can provide a context (sentences/paragraph) for the words and explain their meanings. For building morphological and syntactic knowledge, it is beneficial to provide students with morphological variations of the words in sentences. For the word, *happy*, sentences, such as "The boy was happy, The boy was singing happily, The boy understood the meaning of happiness," can demonstrate how the root word, *happy*, changes its suffix in different sentence structures. It is also recommended that teachers use activities that help students connect all of the aspects of linguistic knowledge (e.g., sentence completion, generating situations that describe the target words).

7.1.1.4 Morphological Awareness

Explicit instruction on how to make use of prefixes and suffixes in word learning is one of the direct methods for promoting morphological awareness (e.g., Baumann et al., 2002; Bellomo, 2009). For example, teachers can explain the meanings of a prefix in words (e.g., *sub* means "below" or "part of") and have students identify where the prefix is in words such as *submarine* and *subcategory*. They can also work on word-meaning inference (e.g., what does *underweight* mean?). Besides explicit instruction, there are several tasks developed for measuring morphological awareness in literacy research, which can be used for instructional purposes. For example, the task developed by Berko (1958), asks students to apply syntactic understanding to complete a sentence. In the sample that follows, students need to be able to add a plural inflectional suffix to the base form, *pax*.

> This is an animal called a pax. Now we have three of them.
> We have three _____. (Answer: *paxes*)

A similar type of fill-in-the-blank task asks students to analyze the syntactic structure and manipulate (add or remove) suffixes in order to complete sentences (e.g., Carlisle, 2000), such as the following.

> *teach*   I want to be a _____. (Answer: *teacher*)
> *happiness* The student was _____. (Answer: *happy*)

Below is a variation of the fill-in-the-blank task with multiple-choice options used in Mahony's study (1994) with English L1 college students. The examples below use a pseudoword, which makes the task more difficult.

> The students participated very _____ in the class today.
>   drintively, drintiveness, drintivism (Answer: drintively)
> The committee finally reached a _____ at the meeting.
>   spetment, spetable, spetableness (Answer: spetment)

Another type of morphological awareness task asks students to identify the root and other morphemes within a word, used by Koda (2000) with college-level ESL students. This is an important skill to develop because students may misunderstand mere orthographic similarity as a derivational morpheme. In the sample shown here, *regroup* can be separated into the prefix, *-re*, and the root, *group*, but *reptile* cannot be separated even though it contains *re* at the word initial position.

> Can the word be separated? – *regroup* (Answer: yes), *reptile* (Answer: no)
> *prepay* (Answer: yes), *pretty* (Answer: no)

A morphological analogy task (Nunes, Bryant, and Bindman, 2006) is a different type of task, in which students are asked to analyze the morphological relationship between A and B, and apply the relationship to C and D in order to find an answer, as shown in the example below.

> A : B :: C : D
> *act* : *action* :: *discuss* : _____ (Answer: *discussion*)
> *beauty*: *beautiful* :: _____ : happy (Answer: *happiness*)

The tasks introduced above are designed for building morphological awareness of derived and inflected words. Compound words require a different set of tasks that draw students' attention to the structure of the head and modifier within a compound. For example, the task used by McBride-Chang et al. (2005) asks children to create a novel compound that matches the definition, as shown in the following example:

> A library has lots of shelves for books. They are a type of shelf, called a bookshelf. A bakery has lots of shelves for bread. What would we call this type of shelf?

In order to come up with the answer (*breadshelf*), students need to analyze the head-modifier structure and the part of speech of the given compound, *bookshelf*, and apply the knowledge to create a new compound. Likewise, a structural analogy task (Zhang et al., 2012) targets the students' understanding of the parts of speech of the root words and asks students to choose the compound that is most similar to the target compound. In the sample shown below, the target word consists of a noun and a noun, which makes the answer *sunhat*.

> Target: *sunroof* Options: sunshine, sundown, sunhat (Answer: sunhat)

7.1.2 Promoting Word Recognition Fluency

Fluency in word recognition is typically measured by speed and accuracy (e.g., Proctor et al., 2005). As described in Chapter 4, fluency (also referred to as automaticity) in word recognition is vital in reading comprehension. Automatic word recognition is rapid and accurate, but effortless, without consuming much of readers' cognitive capacity. With automatic word recognition, readers are able to allocate their cognitive capacity for higher order processing, such as sentence and text comprehension. For the assessment of word recognition ability, a naming task is perhaps the most commonly used. In this task, students read aloud a series of real words and pseudowords (see below for samples) as quickly and accurately as possible.

    some, black, house, exit, time
    frain, ploat, swade, prite, blop

The naming task can be used as a training program for building word recognition fluency. Flashcards, either on paper or a computer, may be used for implementing the task. Similar to metalinguistic awareness in the previous section, word recognition fluency is a crucial skill for developing readers and should be incorporated into instruction for beginning- and intermediate-level students on a regular basis. It may be worthwhile to use a standardized test, such as the Woodcock Reading Mastery Test (Woodcock, 1987), for measuring the students' progress. The rapid automatic naming (RAN) task is another established task for assessing word recognition ability (e.g., Olson, Forsberg, and Wise, 1994). In a version of the RAN task with letters and with numbers, students are asked to name several series of letters or numbers from left to right as rapidly as possible, as shown in the samples here.

    Letters: a d p o s d a o s
    Numbers: 7 2 9 4 6 2 7 4 9

As for L2 studies, there are only a handful that provided word recognition fluency training. One such study is Akamatsu (2008), who provided Japanese L1 ESL students with seven weeks of training on word recognition, using a word chain task. In this task, the students were shown a series of word chains, each of which consisted of five words with no spaces between them (see below for a sample). The task was to draw lines between the words as quickly and accurately as possible.

    Chairthinkflowerlawstreet   (Answer: chair/think/flower/law/street)
    playsnowofficetryclose   (Answer: play/snow/office/try/close)

Another study in L2 word recognition training is by Fukkink, Hulstijn, and Simis (2005). In this study, the researchers administered a computerized training program to Dutch L1 ESL students. The program consisted of four exercises (cloze, square, column, and translation), which intended to provide the students with intensive opportunities to process the target words in sentence contexts. In the cloze exercise, the students were asked to fill in a blank in a sentence, by choosing the correct word from two options. In the square exercise, the target word was shown in the center of the screen, and the students had to indicate whether the combination of the target word and a series of words/phrases shown to them made sense (e.g., burglar—steals; burglar—is welcome). In the column exercise, the students were shown a sentence with a blank and asked to determine whether a given word/phrase fit in the blank (made sense in the sentence). In the translation exercise, the students were shown a sentence with the L1 translation of the target word and chose the correct L2 word from two options.

7.2 Building Reading Comprehension Skills

7.2.1 Promoting Sentence Processing and Interpretation

As in word recognition, promoting automaticity in sentence processing requires building both speed and accuracy in sentence comprehension. As soon as students have some basic vocabulary knowledge and begin reading paragraphs or texts, the sentence-level tasks introduced in this section can be implemented as exercises that promote automaticity in sentence processing and interpretation until the students reach an advanced level of proficiency. Teachers should be aware that students may find it difficult to read phrases and sentences whose structures differ in their L1s.

The Test of Silent Reading Efficiency and Comprehension (Wagner et al., 2010) is a standardized test on sentence processing. In the test, students are asked to read as many sentences as possible in three minutes and indicate whether each sentence is sensible by circling yes or no beside each one. A similar task is grammaticality judgment, a common task used for measuring morpho-syntactic knowledge and sentence processing ability. In the task, students are asked to determine as quickly as possible whether a given sentence is grammatically correct (see more in Chapter 6). The types of sentences vary depending on the targeted morpho-syntactic structures. For example, Gottardo, Siegel, and Stanovich (1997) used sentences that focused on subject-verb-object word order for English L1 adult participants, and Juffs and Harrington (1995) used sentences that focused on wh-movement for Chinese L1 college students. Some sample sentences are provided here. In order to build sentence processing skills, students should be encouraged to make a grammaticality decision as accurately and quickly as possible.

> Was watching the student the football game?
> Was the student watching the football game?
> Which movie did you criticize the man recommended?
> Which movie the man recommended did you criticize?

As for studies that examined the effectiveness of training on sentence processing and comprehension, Weaver (1979) developed sentence anagram training for English L1 third graders. The training aimed to direct children's attention to phrases, rather than single words. They were instructed to look for a verb first and decide which of the remaining words belonged to the same phrase. A sample item is shown in Figure 7.1.

Hulstijn, van Gelderen, and Schoonen (2009) reported a valuable study that examined L2 sentence processing fluency. In the longitudinal part of the study, Dutch-speaking EFL students performed a sentence verification task and a sentence production task three times, at Grades 8, 9, and 10. In the sentence verification task, the students were shown the sentences on a computer screen and asked to decide as quickly as possible whether or not each sentence made sense. The sentences for the "no" answers were grammatically correct but did not make sense in terms of factual knowledge (e.g., most dogs have six legs). In the sentence production task, the students were shown the beginning of a sentence and asked to choose the item that follows. For example, for the beginning part of the sentence, "After some time," the students had to choose the correct answer from the two options, "woke up" or "she."

Figure 7.1 Sample sentence anagram task.

7.2.2 Promoting Reading Comprehension

This section introduces some of the activities and strategies that have been suggested to promote reading comprehension, in particular, comprehension of the main ideas and messages from texts. The activities and strategies are intended to guide students through reading comprehension processes, as they may need to activate background knowledge and apply comprehension strategies. The activities and strategies can be incorporated into reading instruction as pre-reading, during-reading, or post-reading components, depending on their focus.

7.2.2.1 Activating and Supporting Background Knowledge

As described in Chapter 6, readers' background knowledge on the topic of a text plays a crucial role in reading comprehension. Supporting background knowledge is particularly important for L2 students because they generally lack L2 linguistic and cultural knowledge. Before students start reading, it is important that teachers assess their background knowledge in the form of a discussion. For example, Pearson and Spiro (1980) recommend that teachers write down the topic of a text (e.g., photosynthesis) on the board and discuss the associated words/concepts that students come up with. By assessing the associated words/concepts, the teachers can identify how much knowledge the students have regarding the topic.

If students do not have sufficient background knowledge on the topic of a text, it is necessary to build their knowledge through pre-reading activities. For example, Erwin (1991) taught third graders in Texas the words and concepts specific to British culture (e.g., using bed socks and a hot water bottle to keep warm even in the spring), prior to reading a text on the culture. The researcher found that the explicit instruction improved the children's comprehension of the text.

Visuals are an effective tool that can build students' background knowledge. For example, Rance-Roney (2010) created a combination of images, audio, and text (written words/sentences) using digital storytelling technology and also encouraged her students to compose their own digital story as a response to the text they read. Although writing a reflection or response to a text is a common post-reading activity, students who have difficulty in writing may not be able to fully express their thoughts. Sylvester and Greenidge (2009) state that digital storytelling is useful for struggling writers because they can express their thoughts more freely.

There are a number of programmatic approaches that incorporate the activation of background knowledge in the teaching of metacognitive strategies. One well-known approach is the K-W-L approach (Ogle, 1986), which stands for "What students *know*," "What they *want* to know," and "What they have *learned*." In the first stage, K, the students brainstorm their knowledge on a selected topic. In the W stage, they develop their own reasons for reading a text, write down some questions regarding the text, and then read the text. In the final stage, L, the students write down what they learned from reading and evaluate whether their questions have been answered by the text. In the W and L stages, the students are also expected to apply strategies, such as planning and monitoring, to facilitate reading comprehension. Although the approach was originally developed for teaching English L1 children, some studies have confirmed its effectiveness for ESL learners (e.g., Hashemi, Mobini, and Karimkhanlooie, 2016).

Carrell, Pharis, and Liberto (1989) reported that an experience-text-relationship (ETR) approach effectively promoted college-level ESL students' reading comprehension. In the first stage (E), teachers use discussion to activate students' background knowledge about the topic of the text. In the second stage (T), the teachers instruct the students to read short parts of the text and ask questions regarding the parts. In the last stage (R), the students are encouraged to relate the content of the text to their personal experiences and knowledge.

7.2.2.2 Comprehension Strategies

A range of instructional approaches are available for teaching metacognitive strategies for reading comprehension. When teachers model the use of reading comprehension strategies, what they do is to verbalize their thinking processes. The think-aloud technique, which has been used as a research technique, can be used as a pedagogical tool as well.

For example, Klinger, Vaughn, and Schumm (1998) found that collaborative strategic reading, which used the think-aloud technique for teaching comprehension strategies, effectively promoted fourth graders' reading comprehension. A subsequent large-scale study (Boardman et al., 2015), involving two middle schools, confirmed the effectiveness of the approach in promoting reading comprehension. Collaborative strategic reading consists of three stages: preview, reading, and post-reading. In the preview stage, students are asked to look at the title and headings, predict what the text might be about, and brainstorm what they already know about the topic. After the preview, they start reading the first paragraph or section and apply the comprehension strategies, which are click and clunk (identify the difficult parts in comprehension) and get the gist (think about the main point). After reading, the students ask questions about the main point and review what they learned from the text.

Baumann, Seifert-Kessell, and Jones (1992) reported that a directed reading and thinking activity (DRTA) was more effective than using only the think-aloud technique, based on the data from fourth graders. DRTA is a method that combines the think-aloud technique with a predicting strategy. In the pre-reading stage, students make initial predictions about a text from the title and any pictures on the title page, and the teacher writes down their ideas on the board. Next, the students read one-third to one-half of the text and evaluate their initial predictions, by identifying whether they were true, false, partially true, partially false, or not mentioned.

Reciprocal teaching (Palincsar and Brown, 1984) is carried out in a dialog format. A teacher and students read a portion of the text together, during which the teacher models the following four metacognitive strategies: making predictions about a text, questioning their own comprehension, clarifying unclear information in the text, and summarizing the text. After the strategies are introduced, the students continue to read while using the strategies. Although the approach was developed originally for English L1 children, it has also been shown to be effective for ESL learners (e.g., Salataci and Akyel, 2002).

Questioning the author (Beck et al., 1996) is a unique approach that teaches comprehension strategies through asking questions to the author of a text and discussing the answers to the questions. Teachers facilitate questioning the author discussions using a set of queries that have specific goals. For example, the query, "What is the author talking about?" initiates discussion, and "Did the author tell us that?" encourages the students to refer back to the text. These questions are expected to enhance a collaborative conversation between the teachers and students.

Some instructional approaches focus on the teaching of text structures. For example, applying the findings from a meta-analysis (Hebert et al., 2016), Roehling et al. (2017) recommend that teachers provide explicit instruction on the various types of text structures and the words that signal the structures (see some samples here). The researchers state that text-structure instruction is beneficial for promoting comprehension of expository texts, which often include cognitively challenging concepts and are more difficult to comprehend than narrative stories.

> Simple description (e.g., looks like, for example, specifically)
> Compare and contrast (e.g., same as, both, likewise, different, however, but)
> Sequence (e.g., first, second, initially, preceding, before, after)
> Cause and effect (e.g., because, as a result, consequently, therefore)
> Problem and solution (e.g., the problem/issue/difficulty is, solution)

Another tool for teaching text structures is graphic organizers. Studies have shown that graphic organizers facilitate students' reading comprehension in both L1 (Elbro and Buch-Iversen, 2013) and in L2 (Jiang, 2012). It is important to select an appropriate organizer according to the text structure. For example, an organizer for compare-contrast may have two different boxes next to each other for "compare" and "contrast," and an organizer for process and sequence may have each process or step connected with arrows. Jiang and Grabe (2007) illustrate sample graphic organizers for the following text structures: definition, compare-contrast, cause-effect, process and sequence, program-solution, description and classification, argument, for-against, and timeline.

7.3 Word-Meaning Inference Instruction

7.3.1 Instructional Approaches in Word-Meaning Inference

This section introduces some of the approaches that have been shown to be effective for teaching word-meaning inference, although available approaches are still limited. Overall, studies suggest that students benefit from receiving explicit instruction on the steps they should take in inferring the meanings of unknown words. For example, Jenkins, Matlock, and Slocum (1989) implemented the SCANR instruction for English L1 fifth graders, which included five steps: (1) Substitute a word or expression for the unknown word; (2) Check the context for clues that support your idea; (3) Ask yourself if the substitution fits in the entire context; (4) Need a new idea? (double check your work); and (5) Revise the idea to come up with a different word or expression that better fits the context. The teacher practiced these steps with the students using example sentences.

Goerss, Beck, and McKeown (1999) provided word-meaning inference instruction as an intervention for English L1 fifth and sixth graders who were identified as less-skilled readers. The instruction included the following five steps: (1) read and reread while emphasizing the role of the unfamiliar word within the context; (2) discuss the clues to the word's meaning; (3) form an initial hypothesis about the meaning of the unfamiliar word; (4) place constraints on the original idea or develop more hypotheses; and (5) summarize the information from the steps given earlier. In each step, the teacher asked the students specific questions, such as "What is happening in these sentences?" or "What do you think *scowled* might mean?" Answering the questions and discussing them further with the teacher helped the students learn the processes of word-meaning inference.

Buikema and Graves (1993) provided English L1 seventh and eighth graders word-meaning inference instruction in a worksheet format. The first step was to identify unfamiliar words in a text. The students circled/boxed in an unfamiliar word included in the text and wrote down the word. Next, they looked for and wrote down the words and phrases that provided clues to a possible meaning of the word. Then, they were asked to think about a possible meaning of the word and jot down some ideas (e.g., the part of speech of the word, what the word does not mean) before writing down the inferred meaning of the word.

Clarke and Nation (1980) suggest that students use the following four steps in word-meaning inference: (1) determine the part of speech of the unknown word; (2) try to infer the meaning of the unknown word based on the immediate context; (3) narrow down the meaning based on the wider context; and (4) finalize the meaning and evaluate its accuracy (check the part of speech, make use of word-part information, and check it against the context). The researchers also recommend that students analyze conjunction relationships in the wider context in order to narrow down the meaning of the unknown word. The conjunction relationships include the following: inclusion, exclusion, explanation, exemplification, contrast, cause-effect, condition, time, arrangement, summary/conclusion, classification, and comparison.

Explicit explanation of morphological and syntactic cues is commonly incorporated in word-meaning inference instruction, probably due to the fact that it is relatively easy to provide such explanation, given that there are a limited number of rules in morpho-syntactic structures. However, instruction on specific contextual cues is scarce, presumably due to the fact that contextual information is unique to each individual text and more difficult to explain as a set of rules. The conjunction relationships introduced by Clarke and Nation (1980) and the categorization of contextual cues by Sternberg and Powell (1983), including cue types such as temporal, spatial, and stative descriptive (see more in Chapter 2), offer valuable insights into the kinds of contextual cues that can be introduced in instruction.

In order to examine the effect of instruction on a more specific contextual cue, Baumann et al. (2002) provided English L1 fifth graders with instruction on appositives. First, the students learned the definition of appositive and a signal word, such as *or* or *a* (e.g., The principal <u>rescinded</u>, or <u>cancelled</u>, the new dress code). Next, the students were instructed to identify and underline the unfamiliar word and the signal words in practice items. Similarly, Carnine, Kameenui, and Coyle (1984) provided English L1 fourth, fifth, and sixth graders instruction on three contextual cues: synonym, contrast, and inference. The synonym cue included a clear restatement or explanation of a target word, such as "There is a <u>paucity</u> of water in this region. Only <u>very little</u> is available." The contrast cue included an antonym of the target word, such as "There is a <u>paucity</u> of water in this region. It is <u>not enough</u>." The inference cue required the students to infer the meaning of the target word based on an entire sentence, such as "There is a <u>paucity</u> of water in this region. <u>More rain is necessary for growing crops</u>." The researchers found that the synonym cue led to better success than the inference cue.

7.3.2 Recommendations for Word-Meaning Inference Instruction

Finally, this section summarizes the recommendations based on the Cognitive Model of Word-Meaning Inference as well as existing studies in reading and word-meaning inference. Word-meaning inference is a useful method for vocabulary development. However, it is important to note that word-meaning inference is not a flawless method that will always benefit students. Some students may not be able to infer the meanings of unknown words correctly.

Word-meaning inference is suitable for students who have sufficient vocabulary knowledge and reading ability. Students need to know most of the words in a text (ideally, 96–98 percent known-word coverage) and be able to comprehend the text. Therefore, word-meaning inference is not recommended for beginning-level students. For beginning-level students, building bottom-up skills and developing basic vocabulary, up to 3,000 words, is recommended. For students who possess sufficient proficiency, it is recommended that teachers provide explicit instruction on how to infer the meanings of unknown words encountered during reading, including the following steps:

1. Prior to reading and word-meaning inference, students need to look at the title and identify the topic of the text and predict what the text might be about. If they are deemed to lack sufficient background knowledge, a pre-reading activity (e.g., visuals, digital storytelling) is necessary to build their background knowledge. L2 students often lack background knowledge on topics specific to L2 history and culture.
2. Students need to recognize the known and unknown words accurately as they read. When they extract word-form information (orthographic, phonological, and morphological information) from the unknown words, cross-linguistic transfer might affect the quality of the information.
3. Students should analyze the grammar structure of the sentences where the unknown words appear and specify the parts of speech of the unknown words. They can make a preliminary inference of the general meanings of the unknown words (e.g., negative vs. positive meaning, does not mean X, Y, Z). Depending on their L1 morpho-syntactic structures, some sentences may be more difficult to comprehend than others.
4. Students can then read a larger portion of the text and generate global contextual information, while paying attention to the discourse structure of the text as well as making connections to their background knowledge. They should revisit the sentences in which the unknown

words appear and narrow down the inferred meanings of the unknown words.
5. Students should reread the sentences in which the unknown words appear and confirm whether the parts of speech of the inferred meanings match the grammatical structures of the sentences and the morphological information of the unknown words.

Throughout the steps described earlier, students need to approach word-meaning inference in a logical manner, by organizing the information they obtain from the text. The think-aloud technique is a useful strategy for organizing the information. Students also need to monitor and evaluate their performance during reading and word-meaning inference. If they notice that they are not comprehending the text to a satisfactory level or if they think that the text does not provide sufficient contextual information about the meanings of the unknown words, it is recommended that they do not rely on word-meaning inference as the sole method but try a different method, such as using a dictionary.

In order to retain the inferred words' information for the long term, it is recommended that students engage in a follow-up activity, in which they use the words whose meanings they inferred in output production (e.g., discussion, writing). If word-meaning inference is used as a self-learning method outside the classroom, students may follow up with a simple output activity that they can do on their own (e.g., writing down the words they inferred in a journal).

7.4 Chapter Summary

This chapter summarized pedagogical applications based on the Cognitive Model of Word-Meaning Inference. Word recognition and reading comprehension skills are critical for the success of word-meaning inference from reading. For building word recognition skills, which are fundamental for extracting word-form information, instruction should incorporate tasks that develop metalinguistic awareness (orthographic, phonological, and morphological awareness) and word recognition fluency. For building reading comprehension skills, which facilitate the generation of contextual information, instruction should incorporate activities and strategies that promote sentence processing fluency and main idea comprehension. The chapter also introduced instructional approaches to word-meaning inference and offered recommendations for implementing word-meaning inference instruction. The tasks, activities, and strategies introduced in this chapter should provide more tangible tools for learning words from reading.

References

Abu Rabia, S. (1995), "Learning to Read in Arabic: Reading, Syntactic, Orthographic and Working Memory Skills in Normally Achieving and Poor Arabic Readers," *Reading Psychology*, 16: 351–94.

Abu Rabia, S. (1997), "Reading in Arabic Orthography: The Effect of Vowels and Context on Reading Accuracy of Poor and Skilled Native Arabic Readers in Reading Paragraphs, Sentences, and Isolated Words," *Journal of Psycholinguistics Research*, 26: 465–82.

Adams, M. J. (1994), "Modeling the Connections between Word Recognition and Reading," in R. B. Ruddell, M. R. Ruddell and H. Singer (eds.), *Theoretical Models and Processes of Reading*, 4th edn, 830–63, Newark: International Reading Association.

Adolf, S., G. Frishkoff, J. Dandy, and C. Perfetti (2016), "Effects of Induced Orthographic and Semantic Knowledge on Subsequent Learning: A Test of the Partial Knowledge Hypothesis," *Reading and Writing*, 29 (3): 475–500.

Afsharrad, M. and A. R. Sadeghi Benis (2017), "Differences between Monolinguals and Bilinguals/Males and Females in English Reading Comprehension and Strategy Use," *International Journal of Bilingual Education and Bilingualism*, 20 (1): 34–51.

Akamatsu, N. (1999), "The Effects of First Language Orthographic Features on Word Recognition Processing in English as a Second Language," *Reading and Writing*, 11: 381–403.

Akamatsu, N. (2003), "The Effects of First Language Orthographic Features on Second Language Reading in Text," *Language Learning*, 53 (2): 207–31.

Akamatsu, N. (2008), "The Effects of Training on Automatization of Word Recognition in English as a Foreign Language," *Applied Psycholinguistics*, 29: 175–193.

Alderson, J. C. (1984), "Reading in a Foreign Language: A Reading Problem or a Language Problem?," in J. C. Alderson and A. H. Urquhart (eds.), *Reading in a Foreign Language*, 1–24, London: Longman.

Alderson, J. C. (2000), *Assessing Reading*, New York: Cambridge University Press.

Alhaqbani, A. and M. Riazi (2012), "Metacognitive Awareness of Reading Strategy Use in Arabic as a Second Language," *Reading in a Foreign Language*, 24 (2): 231–55.

Alptekin, C. (2006), "Cultural Familiarity in Inferential and Literal Comprehension in L2 Reading," *System*, 34: 494–508.

Anderson, R. C. and P. D. Pearson (1984), "A Schema-Theoretical View of Reading Comprehension," in P. D. Pearson (ed.), *Handbook of Reading Research*, 255–91, New York: Longman.

August, D. and T. Shanahan, eds. (2006), *Developing Literacy in Second-Language Learners: Report of the National Literacy Panel on Language-Minority Children and Youth*, Mahwah: Lawrence Erlbaum.

Baddeley, A., R. Logie and I. Nimmo-Smith (1985), "Components of Fluent Reading," *Journal of Memory and Language*, 24: 119–31.

Baddeley, A. D. (1986), *Working Memory*, Oxford: Oxford University Press.

Barcroft, J. (2009), "Effects of Synonym Generation on Incidental and Intentional L2 Vocabulary Learning during Reading," *TESOL Quarterly*, 43 (1): 79–103.

Barcroft, J. (2015), "Can Retrieval Opportunities Increase Vocabulary Learning during Reading?," *Foreign Language Annals*, 48 (2): 236–49.

Bartolotti, J. and V. Marian (2017), "Orthographic Knowledge and Lexical Form Influence Vocabulary Learning," *Applied Psycholinguistics*, 38: 427–56.

Bates, E. and B. MacWhinney (1989), "Functionalism and the Competition Model," in B. MacWhinney and E. Bates (eds.), *The Cross-Linguistic Study of Sentence Processing*, 3–73, Cambridge: Cambridge University Press.

Baumann, J. F., N. Seifert-Kessell and L. A. Jones (1992), "Effect of Think-Aloud Instruction on Elementary Students' Comprehension Monitoring Abilities," *Journal of Reading Behavior*, 24 (2): 143–72.

Baumann, J. F., E. C. Edwards, G. Font, C. A. Tereshinski, E. J. Kame'enui and S. Olejnik (2002), "Teaching Morphemic and Contextual Analysis to Fifth-Grade Students," *Reading Research Quarterly*, 37 (2): 150–76.

Beck, I. L., M. G. McKeown and E. S. McCaslin (1983), "Vocabulary Development: All Contexts Are not Created Equal," *The Elementary School Journal*, 83 (3): 177–81.

Beck, I. L., M. G. McKeown, C. Sandora, L. Kucan and J. Worthy (1996), "Questioning the Author: A Yearlong Classroom Implementation to Engage Students with Text," *The Elementary School Journal*, 96 (4): 385–414.

Bellomo, T. S. (2009), "Morphological Analysis as a Vocabulary Strategy for L1 and L2 College Preparatory Students," *TESL-EJ*, 13 (3). Available online: https://www.tesl-ej.org/wordpress/issues/volume13/ej51/ej51a1/ (accessed July 12, 2019).

Bensoussan, M. (1998), "Schema Effects in EFL Reading Comprehension," *Journal of Research in Reading*, 21 (3): 213–27.

Bensoussan, M. and B. Laufer (1984), "Lexical Guessing in Context in EFL Reading Comprehension," *Journal of Research in Reading*, 7 (1): 15–32.

Berko, J. (1958), "The Child's Learning of English Morphology," *Word*, 14 (2/3): 150–77.

Bernhardt, E. B. and M. L. Kamil (1995), "Interpreting Relationships between L1 and L2 Reading: Consolidating the Linguistic Threshold and the Linguistic Interdependence Hypotheses," *Applied Linguistics*, 16 (1): 15–34.

Bialystok, E. (2001), *Bilingualism in Development*, Cambridge: Cambridge University Press.

Boardman, A. G., J. K. Klinger, P. Buckley, S. Annamma and C. J. Lasser (2015), "The Efficacy of Collaborative Strategic Reading in Middle School Science and Social Studies Classes," *Reading and Writing*, 28: 1257–83.

Bordag, D., A. Kirschenbaum, M. Rogahn and E. Tschirner (2017), "The Role of Orthotactic Probability in Incidental and Intentional Vocabulary Acquisition L1 and L2," *Second Language Research*, 33 (2): 147–78.

Bowers, J. S., C. J. Davis and D. A. Hanley (2005a), "Automatic Semantic Activation of Embedded Words: Is There a 'hat' in 'that'?," *Journal of Memory and Language*, 52: 131–43.

Bowers, J. S., C. J. Davis and D. A. Hanley (2005b), "Interfering Neighbors: The Impact of Novel Word Learning on the Identification of Visually Similar Words," *Cognition*, 97: B45–54.

Bransford, J. D. and M. K. Johnson (1972), "Contextual Prerequisites for Understanding: Some Investigations of Comprehension and Recall," *Journal of Verbal Learning and Verbal Behavior*, 11 (6): 717–26.

Brantmeier, C. (2005), "Effects of Readers' Knowledge, Text Type, and Test Type on L1 and L2 Reading Comprehension in Spanish," *The Modern Language Journal*, 89: 37–53.

Brown, R., R. Waring and S. Donkaewbua (2008), "Incidental Vocabulary Acquisition from Reading, Reading-while-Listening, and Listening to Stories," *Reading in a Foreign Language*, 20 (2): 136–63.

Brown, T. and M. Haynes (1985), "Literacy Background and Reading Development in a Second Language," in T. H. Carr (ed.), *The Development of Reading Skills*, 19–34, San Francisco: Jossey-Bass.

Brusnighan, S. M., R. K. Morris, J. R. Folk and R. Lowell (2014), "The Role of Phonology in Silent Vocabulary Acquisition during Silent Reading," *Journal of Cognitive Psychology*, 26 (8): 871–92.

Brysbaert, M. and D. C. Mitchell (1996), "Modifier Attachment in Sentence Parsing: Evidence from Dutch," *Quarterly Journal of Experimental Psychology*, 49A: 664–95.

Buikema, J. L. and M. F. Graves (1993), "Teaching Students to Use Context Cues to Infer Word Meanings," *Journal of Reading,* 36 (6): 450–7.

Burgess, A. (1972), *A Clockwork Orange*, Middlesex: Penguin.

Byrne, B. and R. Fielding-Barnsley (1995), "Evaluation of a Program to Teach Phonemic Awareness to Young Children: A 2- and 3-Year Follow-up and a New Preschool Trial," *Journal of Educational Psychology*, 87(3): 488–503.

Cain, K., J. Oakhill and P. Bryant (2004), "Children's Reading Comprehension Ability: Concurrent Prediction by Working Memory, Verbal Ability, and Component Skills," *Journal of Educational Psychology*, 96 (1): 31–42.

Cain, K., J. Oakhill and K. Lemmon (2004), "Individual Differences in the Inference of Word Meanings from Context: The Influence of Reading Comprehension, Vocabulary Knowledge, and Memory Capacity," *Journal of Educational Psychology*, 96 (4): 671–81.

Carlisle, J. F. (2000), "Awareness of the Structure and Meaning of Morphologically Complex Words: Impact on Reading," *Reading and Writing*, 12: 169–90.

Carnine, D., E. J. Kameenui and G. Coyle (1984), "Utilization of Contextual Information in Determining the Meaning of Unfamiliar Words," *Reading Research Quarterly*, 19 (2): 188–204.

Carpenter, P. A. and M. A. Just (1983), "What Your Eyes Do while Your Mind is Reading," in K. Rayner (ed.), *Eye Movements in Reading: Perceptual and Language Processes*, 275–307, New York: Academic Press.

Carr, T. H. and B. A. Levy (1990), *Reading and Its Development: Component Skills Approaches*, San Diego: Academic Press.

Carrell, P. L. (1984a), "Evidence of a Formal Schema in Second Language Comprehension," *Language Learning*, 34 (2): 87–112.

Carrell, P. L. (1984b), "Schema Theory and ESL Reading: Classroom Implications and Applications," *The Modern Language Journal*, 68 (4): 332–43.

Carrell, P. L. (1984c), "The Effects of Rhetorical Organization on ESL Readers," *TESOL Quarterly*, 18 (3): 441–469.

Carrell, P. L., J. Devine and D. E. Eskey, eds. (1988), *Interactive Approaches to Second Language Reading*, Cambridge: Cambridge University Press.

Carrell, P. L. and J. C. Eisterhold (1988), "Schema Theory and ESL Reading Pedagogy," in P. L. Carrell, J. Devine and D. E. Eskey (eds.), *Interactive Approaches to Second Language Reading*, 73–92, Cambridge: Cambridge University Press.

Carrell, P. L., B. G. Pharis and J. C. Liberto (1989), "Metacognitive Strategy Training for ESL Reading," *TESOL Quarterly*, 23 (4): 647–78.

Carson, K. L., G. T. Gillon and T. M. Boustead (2013), "Classroom Phonological Awareness Instruction and Literacy Outcomes in the First Year of School," *Language, Speech, and Hearing Services in Schools*, 44: 147–60.

Carton, A. (1971), "Inferencing: A Process in Using and Learning Language," in P. Pimsleur and T. Quinn (eds.), *The Psychology of Second Language Learning*, 45–58, Cambridge: Cambridge University Press.

Chamot, A. U. and J. M. O'Malley (1994), "Instructional Approaches and Teaching Procedures," in K. Spangenberg-Urbschat and R. Pritchard (eds.), *Kids Come in All Languages: Reading Instruction for ESL Students*, 82–107, Newark: International Reading Association.

Chen, C. and J. Truscott (2010), "The Effects of Repetition and L1 Lexicalization on Incidental Vocabulary Acquisition," *Applied Linguistics*, 31 (5): 693–713.

Chen, C., M. Wang and C. A. Perfetti (2011), "Acquisition of Compound Words in Chinese-English Bilingual Children: Decomposition and Cross-Language Activation," *Applied Psycholinguistics*, 32: 583–600.

Chern, C.-L. (1993), "Chinese Students' Word-Solving Strategies in Reading in English," in T. Huckin, M. Haynes and J. Coady (eds.), *Second Language Reading and Vocabulary Learning*, 67–85, Norwood: Ablex.

Chomsky, N. (1959), "Review of B. F. Skinner's *Verbal Behavior*," *Language*, 35: 26–58.

Chomsky, N. (1975), *Reflections on Language*, New York: Pantheon Books.

Cisero, C. A. and J. M. Royer (1995), "The Development and Cross-Language Transfer of Phonological Awareness," *Contemporary Educational Psychology*, 20: 275–303.

Clahsen, H. and C. Felser (2006), "Grammatical Processing in Language Learners," *Applied Psycholinguistics*, 27: 3–42.

Clarke, D. F. and I. S. P. Nation (1980), "Guessing the Meanings of Words from Context: Strategy and Techniques," *System*, 8: 211–20.

Clarke, M. A. (1980), "The Short Circuit Hypothesis of ESL Reading – or When Language Competence Interferes with Reading Performance," *The Modern Language Journal*, 64 (2): 203–9.

Coady, J. (1993), "Research on ESL/EFL Vocabulary Acquisition: Putting It in Context," in T. Huckin, M. Haynes and J. Coady (eds.), *Second Language Reading and Vocabulary*, 3–23, Westport: Ablex.

Coady, J. (1997), "L2 Vocabulary Acquisition through Extensive Reading," in J. Coady and T. Huckin (eds.), *Second Language Vocabulary Acquisition*, 225–37, Cambridge: Cambridge University Press.

Coltheart, M. (1980), "Reading Phonological Recoding and Deep Dyslexia," in M. Coltheart, K. Patterson and J. C. Marshall (eds.), *Deep Dyslexia*, 197–226, London: Routledge & Kegan Paul.

Coltheart, M. (2007), "Modeling Reading: The Dual-Route Approach," in M. J. Snowling and C. Hulme (eds.), *The Science of Reading: A Handbook*, 6–23, Oxford: Blackwell.

Coltheart, M., K. Rastle, C. Perry and J. Ziegler (2001), "DRC: A Dual Route Cascaded Model of Visual Word Recognition and Reading Aloud," *Psychological Review*, 108 (1): 204–56.

Conroy, M. A. and L. Cupples (2010), "We Could Have Loved and Lost, or We Never Could Have Love at All: Syntactic Misanalysis in L2 Sentence Processing," *Studies in Second Language Acquisition*, 32: 523–52.

Coughlin, C. and A. Tremblay (2013), "Proficiency and Working Memory based Explanations for Nonnative Speakers' Sensitivity to Agreement in Sentence Processing," *Applied Psycholinguistics*, 34: 615–46.

Craik, F. I. M. and R. S. Lockhart (1972), "Levels of Processing: A Framework for Memory Research," *Journal of Verbal Learning and Verbal Behavior*, 11: 671–84.

Crain, S. and D. Shankweiler (1988), "Syntactic Complexity and Reading Acquisition," in A. Davison and G. M. Green (eds.), *Linguistic Complexity and Text Comprehension*, 167–92, Hillsdale: Erlbaum.

Crain, S. and M. J. Steedman (1985), "On not Being Led up the Garden Path: The Use of Context by the Psychological Parser," in D. Dowty, L. Karttunen and A. Zwicky (eds.), *Natural Language Parsing*, 320–58, Cambridge: Cambridge University Press.

Cuetos, F. and D. C. Mitchell (1988), "Cross-Linguistic Differences in Parsing: Restrictions on the Use of the Late Closure Strategy in Spanish," *Cognition*, 30: 73–105.

Cummins, J. (1979), "Linguistic Interdependence and Educational Development of Bilingual Children," *Review of Educational Research*, 49: 222–51.

Cummins, J. (1991), "Interdependence of First- and Second-Language Proficiency in Bilingual Children," in E. Bialystok (ed.), *Language Processing in Bilingual Children*, 70–89, New York: Cambridge University Press.

Cummins, J. (2000), *Language, Power, and Pedagogy: Bilingual Children in the Crossfire*, Philadelphia: Multilingual Matters.

Cunnings, I. (2017), "Parsing and Working Memory in Bilingual Sentence Processing," *Bilingualism: Language and Cognition*, 20 (4): 659–78.

Cziko, G. A. (1980), "Language Competence and Reading Strategies: A Comparison of First- and Second-Language Oral Reading Errors," *Language Learning*, 30: 101–14.

Daneman, M. (1988), "Word Knowledge and Reading Skill," in M. Daneman, G. E. Mackinnon, and T. G. Waller (eds.), *Reading Research: Advances in Theory and Practice*, Vol. 6, 145–75, New York: Academic Press.

Daneman, M. (1991), "Individual Differences in Reading Skills," in R. Barr, M. L. Kamil, P. Mosenthal and P. D. Pearson (eds.), *Handbook of Reading Research*, Vol. 2, 512–38, New York: Longman.

Daneman, M. and P. A. Carpenter (1983), "Individual Differences in Integrating Information between and within Sentences," *Journal of Experimental Psychology: Learning, Memory, and Cognition*, 9 (4): 561–84.

Daneman, M. and I. Green (1986), "Individual Differences in Comprehending and Producing Words in Context," *Journal of Memory and Language*, 25: 1–18.

Davison, A., P. Wilson and G. Hermon (1985), *Effects of Syntactic Connectives and Organizing Cues on Text Comprehension*, Champaign: Center for the Study of Reading.

Day, R. and J. Bamford (1998), *Extensive Reading in the Second Language Classroom*, New York: Cambridge University Press.

Day, R. R., C. Omura and M. Hiramatsu (1991), "Incidental EFL Vocabulary Learning and Reading," *Reading in a Foreign Language*, 7 (2): 541–51.

Day, R. and J. Bamford (2002), "Top Ten Principles for Teaching Extensive Reading," *Reading in a Foreign Language*, 14 (2): 136–41.

de Bot, K., T. S. Paribakht and M. Wesche (1997), "Toward a Lexical Processing Model for the Study of Second Language Vocabulary Acquisition: Evidence from ESL Reading," *Studies in Second Language Acquisition*, 19: 309–29.

de Leeuw, L., E. Segers and L. Verhoeven (2014), "Context, Task, and Reader Effects in Children's Incidental Word Learning from Text," *International Journal of Disability, Development and Education*, 61 (3): 275–87.

Deacon, S. H. (2012), "Sounds, Letters and Meanings: The Independent Influences of Phonological, Morphological and Orthographic Skills on Early Word Reading Accuracy," *Journal of Research in Reading*, 35 (4): 456–75.

Deacon, S. H. and J. R. Kirby (2004), "Morphological Awareness: Just 'More Phonological'? The Roles of Morphological and Phonological Awareness in Reading Development," *Applied Psycholinguistics*, 25: 223–38.

Dekydtspotter, L., Y.-T. Wang, B. Kim, H.-J. Kim, H.-K. Kim and J. K. Lee (2012), "Anaphora under Reconstruction during Processing in English as a Second Language," *Studies in Second Language Acquisition*, 34: 561–90.

Doughty, C. J. (2003), "Instructed SLA: Constraints, Comprehension," in C. J. Doughty and M. H. Long (eds.), *The Handbook of Second Language Acquisition*, 256–310, Malden: Blackwell.

Duñabeitia, J. A., M. Carreiras and M. Perea (2008), "Are Coffee and Toffee Served in a Cup? Orthophonologically Mediated Associative Priming," *Quarterly Journal of Experimental Psychology*, 61: 1861–72.

Dupuy, B. and S. D. Krashen (1993), "Incidental Vocabulary Acquisition in French as a Foreign Language," *Applied Language Learning*, 4 (1 & 2): 55–63.

Dupuy, H. (1974), *The Rationale, Development and Standardization of a Basic Word Vocabulary Test*, Washington, DC: U. S. Government Printing Office (DHEW Publication No. HRA 74-1334).

Durgunoğlu, A. Y., W. E. Nagy and B. J. Hancin-Bhatt (1993), "Cross-Language Transfer of Phonological Awareness," *Journal of Educational Psychology*, 85 (3): 453–65.

Durso, F. T. and W. J. Shore (1991), "Partial Knowledge of Word Meanings," *Journal of Experimental Psychology: General*, 120 (2): 190–202.

Echevarria, J., M. Vogt, and D. Short (2013), *Making Content Comprehensible for English Learners: The SIOP Model*, 3rd edn, Boston: Pearson.

Eckerth, J. and P. Tavakoli (2012), "The Effects of Word Exposure Frequency and Elaboration of Word Processing on Incidental L2 Vocabulary Acquisition through Reading," *Language Teaching Research*, 16 (2): 227–52.

Ehri, L. C. (1995), "Phases of Development in Learning to Read Words by Sight," *Journal of Research in Reading*, 18 (2): 116–25.

Ehri, L. C. (1998), "Grapheme-Phoneme Knowledge is Essential to Learning to Read Words in English,' in J. L. Metsala and L. C. Ehri (eds.), *Word Recognition in Beginning Literacy*, 3–40, Mahwah: Erlbaum.

Elbro, C. and I. Buch-Iversen (2013), "Activation of Background Knowledge for Inference Making: Effects on Reading Comprehension," *Scientific Studies of Reading*, 17 (6): 435–52.

Elgort, I., S. Candry, T. J. Boutorwick, J. Eyckmans and M. Brysbaert (2018), "Contextual Word Learning with Form-Focused and Meaning-Focused Elaboration," *Applied Linguistics*, 39 (5): 646–67.

Elley, W. B. and F. Mangubhai (1983), "The Impact of Reading on Second Language Learning," *Reading Research Quarterly*, 19 (1): 53–67.

Ellis, N. C. and A. Beaton (1993), "Psycholinguistic Determinants of Foreign Language Vocabulary Learning," *Language Learning*, 43: 559–617.

Ender, A. (2016), "Implicit and Explicit Cognitive Processes in Incidental Vocabulary Acquisition," *Applied Linguistics*, 37 (4): 536–60.

Erçetin, G. and C. Alptekin (2013), "The Explicit/Implicit Knowledge Distinction and Working Memory: Implications for Second-Language Reading Comprehension," *Applied Psycholinguistics*, 34: 727–53.

Ericsson, L. and H. Simon (1984), *Protocol Analysis: Verbal Reports as Data*, Cambridge: Cambridge University Press.

Erwin, B. (1991), "The Relationship between Background Experience and Students' Comprehension: A Cross Cultural Study," *Reading Psychology*, 12: 43–61.

Felser, C., L. Roberts, T. Marinis and R. Gross (2003), "The Processing of Ambiguous Sentences by First and Second Language Learners of English," *Applied Psycholinguistics*, 24: 453–89.

Felser, C. and L. Roberts (2007), "Processing *Wh*-Dependencies in a Second Language: A Cross-Modal Priming Study," *Second Language Research*, 23 (1): 9–36.

Fender, M. (2003), "English Word Recognition and Word Integration Skills of Native Arabic- and Japanese-Speaking Learners of English as a Second Language," *Applied Psycholinguistics*, 24: 289–315.

Ferreira, F. and C. Clifton, Jr. (1986), "The Independence of Syntactic Processing," *Journal of Memory and Language*, 25: 348–68.
Foroodi-Nejad, F. and J. Paradis (2009), "Crosslinguistic Transfer in the Acquisition of Compound Words in Persian-English Bilinguals," *Bilingualism: Language and Cognition*, 12 (4): 411–27.
Fowler, C. A., S. E. Napps and L. Feldman (1985), "Relations Among Regular and Irregular Morphologically Related Words in the Lexicon as Revealed by Repetition Priming," *Memory and Cognition*, 13: 241–55.
Frantzen, D. (2003), "Factors Affecting How Second Language Spanish Students Derive Meaning from Context," *The Modern Language Journal*, 87 (2): 168–99.
Fraser, C. A. (1999), "Lexical Processing Strategy Use and Vocabulary Learning through Reading," *Studies in Second Language Acquisition*, 21: 225–41.
Frazier, L. (1987), "Sentence Processing: A Tutorial Review," in M. Coltheart (ed.), *Attention and Performance XII: The Psychology of Reading*, 559–86, Hove: Erlbaum.
French-Mestre, C. and J. Pynte (1997), "Syntactic Ambiguity Resolution while Reading in Second and Native Languages," *The Quarterly Journal of Experimental Psychology*, 50A (1): 119–48.
Frost, R., L. Katz and S. Bentin (1987), "Strategies for Visual Word Recognition and Orthographical Depth: A Multilingual Comparison," *Journal of Experimental Psychology: Human Perception and Performance*, 13 (1): 104–15.
Fukkink, R. G., J. Hulstijn and A. Simis (2005), "Does Training in Second-Language Word Recognition Skills Affect Reading Comprehension? An Experimental Study," *The Modern Language Journal*, 89 (1): 54–75.
Gagné, C. L. and E. J. Shoben (1997), "Influence of Thematic Relations on the Comprehension of Modifier-Noun Combinations," *Journal of Experimental Psychology: Learning, Memory, and Cognition*, 23 (1): 71–87.
Garan, E. M. and G. DeVoogd (2008), "The Benefits of Sustained Silent Reading: Scientific Research and Common Sense Converge," *The Reading Teacher*, 62 (4): 336–44.
Gass, S. (1999), "Discussion: Incidental Vocabulary Learning," *Studies in Second Language Acquisition*, 21: 319–33.
Gass, S. M. and L. Selinker, eds. (1983), *Language Transfer in Language Learning*, Rowley: Newbury House.
Gathercole, S. E., G. J. Hitch, A.-M. Adams and A. J. Martin (1999), "Phonological Short-Term Memory and Vocabulary Development: Further Evidence on the Nature of the Relationship," *Applied Cognitive Psychology*, 13: 65–77.
Geva, E., K. Galili, T. Katzir and M. Shany (2017), "Learning Novel Words by Ear or by Eye? An Advantage for Lexical Inferencing in Listening versus Reading Narratives in Fourth Grade," *Reading and Writing*, 30: 1917–44.

Godfroid, A., F. Boers and A. Housen (2013), "An Eye for Words: Gauging the Role of Attention in Incidental L2 Vocabulary Acquisition by Means of Eye-Tracking," *Studies in Second Language Acquisition*, 35: 483–517.

Godfroid, A., J. Ahn, A. Choi, L. Ballard, Y. Cui, S. Johnston, S. Lee, A. Sarkar and H.-J. Yoon (2018), "Incidental Vocabulary Learning in a Natural Reading Context: An Eye-Tracking Study," *Bilingualism: Language and Cognition*, 21 (3): 563–84.

Goerss, B. L., I. L. Beck and M. G. McKeown (1999), "Increasing Remedial Students' Ability to Derive Word Meaning from Context," *Journal of Reading Psychology*, 20: 151–75.

Goldsmith-Phillips, J. (1989), "Word and Context in Reading Development: A Test of the Interactive-Compensatory Hypothesis," *Journal of Educational Psychology*, 81 (3): 299–305.

Goodman, K. S. (1967), "Reading: A Psycholinguistic Guessing Game," *Journal of the Reading Specialist*, 6 (1): 126–35.

Goodman, K. S. (1970), "Psycholinguistic Universals in the Reading Process," *Journal of Typographic Research*, 4 (2): 103–10.

Goswami, U. and P. Bryant (1990), *Phonological Skills and Learning to Read: Essays in Developmental Psychology Series*, Hove: Psychology Press.

Gottardo, A., L. S. Siegel and K. E. Stanovich (1997), "The Assessment of Adults with Reading Disabilities: What Can We Learn from Experimental Tasks?," *Journal of Research in Reading*, 20 (1): 42–54.

Gottardo, A., A. Pasquarella, X. Chen and G. Ramirez (2016), "The Impact of Language on the Relationships between Phonological Awareness and Word Reading in Different Orthographies: A Test of the Psycholinguistic Grain Size Theory in Bilinguals," *Applied Psycholinguistics*, 37: 1083–115.

Gough, P. B. (1972), "One Second of Reading," in J. F. Kavanagh and I. G. Mattingly (eds.), *Language by Ear and by Eye: The Relationship between Speech and Reading*, 331–58, Cambridge, MA: MIT Press.

Gough, P. B. (1996), "How Children Learn to Read and Why They Fail," *Annals of Dyslexia*, 46: 3–20.

Gough, P. B. and C. Juel (1991), "The First Stages of Word Recognition," in L. Rieben and C. A. Perfetti (eds.), *Learning to Read: Basic Research and Its Implications*, 47–56, Hillsdale: Erlbaum.

Gough, P. B. and W. E. Tunmer (1986), "Decoding, Reading, and Reading Disability," *RASE: Remedial and Special Education*, 7 (1), 6–10.

Grabe, W. (2009), *Reading in a Second Language: Moving from Theory to Practice*, New York: Cambridge University Press.

Grabe, W. and F. L. Stoller (2011), *Teaching and Researching Reading*, 2nd edn, New York: Routledge.

Green, D. and P. Meara (1987), "The Effects of Script on Visual Search," *Second Language Research*, 3: 102–17.

Green, D., P. Meara and S. Court (1989), "Are Numbers Logographs?," *Journal of Research in Reading*, 12: 49–58.

Greenberg, D., V. Rodrigo, A. Berry, T. Brinck and H. Joseph (2006), "Implementation of an Extensive Reading Program with Adult Learners," *Adult Basic Education*, 16 (2): 81–97.

Haastrup, K. (1991), *Lexical Inferencing Procedures or Talking about Words: Receptive Procedures in Foreign Language Learning with Special Reference to English*, Tübingen: Gunter Narr.

Hamada, M. (2014), "The Role of Morphological and Contextual Information in L2 Lexical Inference," *The Modern Language Journal*, 98 (4): 992–1005.

Hamada, M. (2017), "L2 Word Recognition: Influence of L1 Orthography on Multi-Syllabic Word Recognition," *Journal of Psycholinguistic Research*, 46: 1101–18.

Hamada, M. and K. Koda (2008), "Influence of First Language Orthographic Experience on Second Language Decoding and Word Learning," *Language Learning*, 58 (1): 1–31.

Hamada, M. and K. Koda (2010), "The Role of Phonological Decoding in Second Language Word-Meaning Inference," *Applied Linguistics*, 31 (4): 513–31.

Hamada, M. and K. Koda (2011), "Similarity and Difference in Learning L2 Word-Form," *System*, 39: 500–9.

Han, A. and C.-L. A. Chen (2010), "Repeated-Reading-Based Instructional Strategy and Vocabulary Acquisition: A Case Study of a Heritage Speaker of Chinese," *Reading in a Foreign Language*, 22 (2): 242–62.

Harm, M. W. and M. S. Seidenberg (2004), "Computing the Meanings of Words in reading: Cooperative Division of Labor Between Visual and Phonological Processes," *Psychological Review*, 111 (3): 662–720.

Hashemi, A., F. Mobini and G. Karimkhanlooie (2016), "The Impact of Content-Based Pre-Reading Activities on Iranian High School EFL Learners' Reading Comprehension," *Journal of Language Teaching and Research*, 7 (1): 137–45.

Hayashi, Y. and V. A. Murphy (2013), "On the Nature of Morphological Awareness in Japanese-English Bilingual Children: A Cross-Linguistic Perspective," *Bilingualism: Language and Cognition*, 16 (1): 49–67.

Hayes-Harb, R. (2006), "Native Speakers of Arabic and ESL Texts: Evidence for the Transfer of Written Word Identification Processes," *TESOL Quarterly*, 40 (2): 321–39.

Haynes, M. (1993), "Patterns and Perils of Guessing in Second Language Reading," in T. Huckin, M. Haynes and J. Coady (eds.), *Second Language Reading and Vocabulary Learning*, 46–64, Norwood: Ablex.

Hebert, M., J. J. Bohaty, J. R. Nelson and J. Brown (2016), "The Effects of Text Structure Instruction on Expository Reading Comprehension: A Meta-Analysis," *Journal of Educational Psychology*, 108 (5): 609–29.

Henriksen, B. (1999), "Three Dimensions of Vocabulary Development," *Studies in Second Language Acquisition*, 21: 303–17.

Hersch, J. and S. Andrews (2012), "Lexical Quality and Reading Skill: Bottom-Up and Top-Down Contributions to Sentence Processing," *Scientific Studies of Reading*, 16 (3): 240–62.

Hill, M. and B. Laufer (2003), "Type of Task, Time-on-Task and Electronic Dictionaries in Incidental Vocabulary Acquisition," *IRAL*, 42: 87–106.

Hirsh, D. and P. Nation (1992), "What Vocabulary Size is Needed to Read Unsimplified Texts for Pleasure?," *Reading in a Foreign Language*, 8 (2): 689–96.

Holmes, V. M. and J. Carruthers (1998), "The Relation between Reading and Spelling in Skilled Adult Readers," *Journal of Memory and Language*, 39: 264–89.

Hoover, W. A. and P. B. Gough (1990), "The Simple View of Reading," *Reading and Writing*, 2: 127–60.

Horiba, Y. (1996), "Comprehension Processes in L2 Reading: Language Competence, Textual Coherence, and Inferences," *Studies in Second Language Acquisition*, 18: 433–73.

Horiba, Y. and K. Fukaya (2015), "Reading and Learning from L2 Text: Effects of Reading Goal, Topic Familiarity, and Language Proficiency," *Reading in a Foreign Language*, 27 (1): 22–46.

Horst, M. (2005), "Learning L2 Vocabulary Through Extensive Reading: A Measurement Study," *The Canadian Modern Language Review*, 61 (3): 355–82.

Horst, M., T. Cobb and T. Meara (1998), "Beyond a Clockwork Orange: Acquiring Second Language Vocabulary Through Reading," *Reading in a Foreign Language*, 11 (2): 207–23.

Hu, H.-C. M. and H. Nassaji (2012), "Ease of Inferencing, Learner Inferential Strategies, and Their Relationship with the Retention of Word Meanings Inferred from Context," *The Canadian Modern Language Review*, 68 (1): 54–77.

Hu, H.-C. M. and H. Nassaji (2014), "Lexical Inferencing Strategies: The Case of Successful Versus Less Successful Inferencers," *System*, 45: 27–38.

Hu, H.-C. M. and P. Nation (2000), "Unknown Vocabulary Density and Reading Comprehension," *Reading in a Foreign Language*, 13 (1): 403–30.

Huang, S., Z. Eslami and V. Wilson (2012), "The Effects of Task Involvement Load on L2 Incidental Vocabulary Learning: A Meta-Analytic Study," *The Modern Language Journal*, 96 (4): 544–57.

Huckin, T. and J. Block (1993), "Strategies for Inferring Word Meaning in Context: A Cognitive Model," in T. Huckin, M. Haynes and J. Coady (eds.), *Second Language Reading and Vocabulary*, 153–78, Westport: Ablex.

Huckin, T. and J. Coady (1999), "Incidental Vocabulary Acquisition in a Second Language: A Review," *Studies in Second Language Acquisition*, 21: 181–93.

Huffman, J. (2014), "Reading Rate Gains during a One-Semester Extensive Reading Course," *Reading in a Foreign Language*, 26 (2): 17–33.

Hulstijn, J. H. (1992), "Retention of Inferred and Given Word Meanings: Experiments in Incidental Vocabulary Learning," in P. J. L. Arnaud and H. Béjoint (eds.), *Vocabulary and Applied Linguistics*, 113–25, Basingstoke: Macmillan.

Hulstijn, J. H. (2003), "Incidental Intentional Learning," in C. J. Doughty and M. H. Long (eds.), *The Handbook of Second Language Acquisition*, 349–408, Malden: Blackwell.

Hulstijn, J. H., M. Hollander and T. Greidanus (1996), "Incidental Vocabulary Learning by Advanced Foreign Language Students: The Influence of Marginal Glosses, Dictionary Use, and Reoccurrence of Unknown Words," *The Modern Language Journal*, 80 (3): 327–39.

Hulstijn, J. H. and B. Laufer (2001), "Some Empirical Evidence for the Involvement Load Hypothesis in Vocabulary Acquisition," *Language Learning*, 51: 539–58.

Hulstijn, J. H., A. van Gelderen and R. Schoonen (2009), "Automatization in Second Language Acquisition: What Does the Coefficient of Variation Tell Us?," *Applied Psycholinguistics*, 30: 555–82.

Inagaki, S. (2001), "Motion Verbs with Goal PPs in the L2 Acquisition of English and Japanese," *Studies in Second Language Acquisition*, 23: 153–70.

Inagaki, S. (2002), "Japanese Learners' Acquisition of English Manner-of-Motion Verbs with Locational/Directional PPs," *Second Language Research*, 18 (1): 3–27.

Jegerski, J., B. van Pattern and G. D. Keating (2011), "Cross-Linguistic Variation and the Acquisition of Pronominal Reference in L2 Spanish," *Second Language Research*, 27 (4): 481–507.

Jenkin, H., S. Prior, R. Rinaldo, A. Wainwright-Sharp and E. Bialystok (1993), "Understanding Text in a Second Language: A Psychological Approach to an SLA Problem," *Second Language Research*, 9 (2): 118–39.

Jenkins, J. R. and R. Dixon (1983), "Vocabulary Learning," *Contemporary Educational Psychology*, 8: 237–60.

Jenkins, J. R., M. L. Stein and K. Wysocki (1984), "Learning Vocabulary through Reading," *American Educational Research Journal*, 21 (4): 767–87.

Jenkins, J. R., B. Matlock and T. A. Slocum (1989), "Two Approaches to Vocabulary Instruction: The Teaching of Individual Word Meanings and Practice in Deriving Word Meaning from Context," *Reading Research Quarterly*, 24 (2): 215–35.

Jeon, E. H. (2011), "Contribution of Morphological Awareness to Second-Language Reading Comprehension," *The Modern Language Journal*, 95 (2): 217–35.

Jeon, E. H. and J. Yamashita (2014), "L2 Reading Comprehension and Its Correlates: A Meta-Analysis," *Language Learning*, 64 (1): 160–12.

Jiang, N. (2002), "Form-Meaning Mapping in Vocabulary Acquisition in a Second Language," *Studies in Second Language Acquisition*, 24: 617–37.

Jiang, N. (2004), "Morphological Insensitivity in Second Language Processing," *Applied Psycholinguistics*, 25: 603–34.

Jiang, N. (2007), "Selective Integration of Linguistic Knowledge in Adult Second Language Learning," *Language Learning*, 57 (1): 1–33.

Jiang, X. (2012), "Effects of Discourse Structure Graphic Organizers on EFL Reading Comprehension," *Reading in a Foreign Language*, 24 (1): 84–105.

Jiang, X. and W. Grabe (2007), "Graphic Organizers in Reading Instruction: Research Findings and Issues," *Reading in a Foreign Language*, 19 (1): 34–55.

Joe, A. (1995), "Text-Based Tasks and Incidental Vocabulary Learning," *Second Language Research*, 11 (2): 149–58.

Joe, A. (1998), "What Effects Do Text-Based Tasks Promoting Generation Have on Incidental Vocabulary Acquisition?," *Applied Linguistics*, 19 (3): 357–77.

Joh, J. and L. Plakans (2017), "Working Memory in L2 Reading Comprehension: The Influence of Prior Knowledge," *System*, 70: 107–20.

Johnson-Laird, P. N. (1983), *Mental Models*, Cambridge, MA: Harvard University Press.

Jones, L. (1979), *Simplified Version of T. Hardy's The Mayor of Casterbridge, 2000 Basewords*, Walton-on-Thames: Nelson.

Juffs, A. and M. Harrington (1995), "Parsing Effects in Second Language Sentence Processing: Subject and Object Asymmetries in Wh-Extraction," *Studies in Second Language Acquisition*, 17: 483–516.

Juffs, A. (1998), "Main Verb Versus Reduced Relative Clause Ambiguity Resolution in L2 Sentence Processing," *Language Learning*, 48 (1): 107–47.

Just, M. A. and P. A. Carpenter (1980), "A Theory of Reading: From Eye Fixations to Comprehension," *Psychological Review*, 87 (4): 329–54.

Kaan, E., J. C. Ballantyne and F. Wijnen (2015), "Effects of Reading Speed on Second-Language Sentence Processing," *Applied Psycholinguistics*, 36: 799–830.

Kaplan, R. B. (1966), "Cultural Thought Patterns in Intercultural Education," *Language Learning*, 16 (1–2): 1–20.

Kaplan, R. B. (1988), "Contrastive Rhetoric and Second Language Learning: Notes Towards a Theory of Contrastive Rhetoric," in A. C. Purves (ed.), *Writing Across Languages and Cultures: Issues in Contrastive Rhetoric*, 275–304, Newbury Park: Sage.

Kellerman, E. and M. Sharwood Smith, eds. (1986), *Crosslinguistic Influence in Second Language Acquisition*, New York: Pergamon Press.

Kern, R. G. (1989), "Second Language Reading Strategy Instruction: Its Effects on Comprehension and Word Inference Ability," *The Modern Language Journal*, 73 (2): 135–49.

Kieffer, M. J., G. Biancarosa and J. Mancilla-Martinez (2013), "Roles of Morphological Awareness in the Reading Comprehension of Spanish-Speaking Language Minority Learners: Exploring Partial Mediation by Vocabulary and Reading Fluency," *Applied Psycholinguistics*, 34: 697–725.

Kilborn, K. (1989), "Sentence Processing in a Second Language: The Timing of Transfer," *Language and Speech*, 32 (1): 1–23.

Kim, Y. H. and E. T. Goetz (1994), "Context Effects on Word Recognition and Reading Comprehension of Poor and Good Readers: A Test of the Interactive-Compensatory Hypothesis," *Reading Research Quarterly*, 29 (1): 179–88.

Kintsch, W. (1988), "The Use of Knowledge in Discourse Processing: A Construction-Integration Model," *Psychological Review*, 95: 163–2.

Kintsch, W. (1998), *Comprehension: A Paradigm for Cognition*, New York: Cambridge University Press.

Klinger, J. K., S. Vaughn and J. S. Schumm (1998), "Collaborative Strategic Reading during Social Studies in Heterogeneous Fourth-Grade Classrooms," *The Elementary School Journal*, 99 (1): 3–22.

Knight, S. (1994), "Dictionary Use while Reading: The Effects on Comprehension and Vocabulary Acquisition for Students of Different Verbal Abilities," *The Modern Language Journal*, 78 (3): 285–99.

Ko, I. Y., M. Wang and S. Y. Kim (2011), "Bilingual Reading of Compounds," *Journal of Psycholinguistics Research*, 40: 49–73.

Koda, K. (1989), "Effects of L1 Orthographic Representation on L1 Phonological Coding Strategies," *Journal of Psycholinguistic Research*, 18: 201–22.

Koda, K. (2000), "Cross-Linguistic Variations in L2 Morphological Awareness," *Applied Psycholinguistics*, 21: 297–320.

Koda, K. (2005), *Insights into Second Language Reading: A Cross-Linguistic Approach*, Cambridge: Cambridge University Press.

Koda, K. (2007), "Reading and Language Learning: Crosslinguistic Constraints on Second Language Reading Development," *Language Learning*, 57 (Suppl. 1): 1–44.

Kondo-Brown, K. (2006), "How Do English L1 Learners of Advanced Japanese Infer Unknown Kanji Words in Authentic Texts?," *Language Learning*, 56 (1): 109–53.

Konopak, K., C. Sheard, D. Longman, B. Lyman, E. Slaton, R. Atkinson and D. Thames (1987), "Incidental Versus Intentional Word Learning from Context," *Reading Psychology*, 8 (1): 7–21.

Krashen, S. (1981), *Second Language Acquisition and Second Language Learning*, Oxford: Pergamon.

Krashen, S. (1982), *Principles and Practice in Second Language Acquisition*, Oxford: Pergamon.

Krashen, S. (1985), *The Input Hypothesis: Issues and Implications*, Harlow: Longman.

Krashen, S. (1989), "We Acquire Vocabulary and Spelling by Reading: Additional Evidence for the Input Hypothesis," *The Modern Language Journal*, 73: 440–64.

Krashen, S. D. (1993), "The Case for Free Voluntary Reading," *The Canadian Modern Language Review*, 50 (1): 72–82.

Kucan, L. (2012), "What Is Most Important to Know about Vocabulary?," *The Reading Teacher*, 65 (6): 360–6.

Kuhn, M. R. and S. A. Stahl (1998), "Teaching Children to Learn Word Meanings from Context: A Synthesis and Some Questions," *Journal of Literacy Research*, 30 (1): 119–38.

Kweon, S.-O. and H.-R. Kim (2008), "Beyond Raw Frequency: Incidental Vocabulary Acquisition in Extensive Reading," *Reading in a Foreign Language*, 20 (2): 191–215.

LaBerge, D. and S. J. Samuels (1974), "Toward a Theory of Automatic Information Processing in Reading," *Cognitive Psychology*, 6: 293–323.

Laufer, B. (1992), "How Much Lexis Is Necessary for Reading Comprehension?," in P. J. L. Arnaud and H. Béjoint (eds.), *Vocabulary and Applied Linguistics*, 126–32, London: Palgrave McMillan.

Laufer, B. (2005), "Focus on Form in Second Language Vocabulary Learning," *EUROSLA Yearbook*, 5: 223–50.

Laufer, B. (2006), "Comparing Focus on Form and Focus on FormS in Second-Language Vocabulary Learning," *The Canadian Modern Language Review*, 63 (1): 149–66.

Laufer, B. (2010), "Form-Focused Instruction in Second Language Vocabulary," in R. Chacón-Beltrán, C. Abello-Contesse and M. D. M. Torreblanca-López (eds.), *Insights into Non-Native Vocabulary Teaching and Learning*, 15–27, Bristol: Multilingual Matters.

Laufer, B. and J. Hulstijn (2001), "Incidental Vocabulary Acquisition in a Second Language: The Construct of Task-Induced Involvement," *Applied Linguistics*, 22 (1): 1–26.

Laufer, B. and B. Rozovski-Roitblat (2011), "Incidental Vocabulary Acquisition: The Effects of Task Type, Word Occurrence and Their Combination," *Language Teaching Research*, 15 (4): 391–411.

Laufer, B. and B. Rozovski-Roitblat (2015), "Retention of New Words: Quantity of Encounters, Quality of Task, and Degree of Knowledge," *Language Teaching Research*, 19 (6): 687–711.

Lee, S.-K. (2009), "Topic Congruence and Topic Interest: How Do They Affect Second Language Reading Comprehension?," *Reading in a Foreign Language*, 21 (2): 159–78.

Lee, V. (2011), "Becoming the Reading Mentors Our Adolescents Deserve: Developing a Successful Sustained Silent Reading Program," *Journal of Adolescent and Adult Literacy*, 55 (3): 209–18.

Lee-Daniels, S. L. and B. A. Murray (2000), "DEAR Me: What Does It Take to Get Children Reading?," *The Reading Teacher*, 54 (2): 154–9.

Leeser, M. J. (2007), "Learner-Based Factors in L2 Reading Comprehension and Processing Grammatical Form: Topic Familiarity and Working Memory," *Language Learning*, 57 (2): 229–70.

Lesgold, A. M. and C. A. Perfetti (1981), *Interactive Processes in Reading*, Hillsdale: Lawrence Erlbaum Associates.

Leung, C. Y. (2002), "Extensive Reading and Language Learning: A Diary Study of a Beginning Learner of Japanese," *Reading in a Foreign Language*, 14 (1): 66–81.

Levelt, W. J. M. (1989), *Speaking: From Intention to Articulation*, Cambridge, MA: MIT Press.

Li, M., N. Jiang and J. Gor (2017), "L1 and L2 Processing of Compound Words: Evidence from Masked Priming Experiments in English," *Bilingualism: Language and Cognition*, 20 (2): 384–402.

Libben, G. (1998), "Semantic Transparency in the Processing of Compounds: Consequences for Representation, Processing, and Impairment," *Brain and Language*, 61: 30–44.

Libben, G., M. Gibson, Y. B. Yoon and D. Sandra (2003), "Compound Fracture: The Role of Semantic Transparency and Morphological Headedness," *Brain and Language*, 84: 50–64.

Liberman, I. Y. and D. Shankweiler (1991), "Phonology and Beginning Reading: A Tutorial," in L. Rieben and C. A. Perfetti (eds.), *Learning to Read: Basic Research and Its Implications*, 3–17, Hillsdale: Lawrence Erlbaum.

Lim, J. H. and K. Christianson (2013), "Second Language Sentence Processing in Reading for Comprehension and Translation," *Bilingualism: Language and Cognition*, 16 (3): 518–37.

Liow, S. J. R., D. Green and M. M. L.-J. Tam (1999), "The Development of Visual Search Strategies in Biscriptal Readers," *The International Journal of Bilingualism*, 3: 333–49.

Liu, N. and I. S. P. Nation (1985), "Factors Affecting Guessing Vocabulary in Context," *RELC Journal*, 16: 33–42.

Lockett, J. N. and W. J. Shore (2003), "A Narwhal is an Animal: Partial Word Knowledge Biases Adults' Decisions," *Journal of Psycholinguistic Research*, 32 (4): 477–96.

Long, M. (1991), "Focus on Form: A Design Feature in Language Teaching Methodology," in K. de Bot, R. Ginsberg and C. Kramsh (eds.), *Foreign Language Research in Cross-Cultural Perspective*, 39–52, Amsterdam: John Benjamins.

Mahony, D. L. (1994), "Using Sensitivity to Word Structure to Explain Variance in High School and College Level Reading Ability," *Reading and Writing*, 6: 19–44.

Manis, F. R., P. A. Szeszulski, L. K. Holt and K. Graves (1990), "Variation in Competent Word Recognition and Spelling Skills among Dyslexic Children and Normal Readers," in T. Carr and B. Levy (eds.), *Reading and Its Development: Component Skills Approaches*, 207–59, San Diego: Academic Press.

Mann, V. A. (1991), "Phonological Abilities: Effective Predictions of Future Reading Ability," in L. Rieben and C. A. Perfetti (eds.), *Learning to Read: Basic Research and Its Implications*, 121–33, Hillsdale: Erlbaum.

Mazuka, R. and K. Itoh (1995), "Can Japanese Speakers Be Led down the Garden Path?," in R. Mazuka and N. Nagai (eds.), *Japanese Sentence Processing*, 295–330, Hillsdale: Erlbaum.

McBride-Chang, C., R. K. Wagner, A. Muse, B. W.-Y. Chow and H. Shu (2005), "The Role of Morphological Awareness in Children's Vocabulary Acquisition in English," *Applied Psycholinguistics*, 26: 415–35.

McCarthy, M. J. (1990), *Vocabulary*, Oxford: Oxford University Press.

McCutchen, D. and B. Logan (2011), "Inside Incidental Word Learning: Children's Strategic Use of Morphological Information to Infer Word Meanings," *Reading Research Quarterly*, 46: 334–49.

McDonald, M. C., N. J. Pearlmutter and M. S. Seidenberg (1994), "The Lexical Nature of Syntactic Ambiguity Resolution," *Psychological Review*, 101: 676–703.

McKoon, G. and R. Ratcliff (1981), "The Comprehension Processes and Memory Structures Involved in Instrumental Inference," *Journal of Verbal Learning and Verbal Behavior*, 20: 671–82.

McNeil, L. (2011), "Investigating the Contributions of Background Knowledge and Reading Comprehension Strategies to L2 Reading Comprehension: An Exploratory Study," *Reading and Writing*, 24: 883–902.

Meara, P. (1997), "Towards a New Approach to Modelling Vocabulary Acquisition," in N. Schmitt and M. McCarthy (eds.), *Vocabulary: Description, Acquisition and Pedagogy*, 109–21, Cambridge: Cambridge University Press.

Mimeau, C., J. Ricketts and S. H. Deacon (2018), "The Role of Orthographic and Semantic Learning in Word Reading and Reading Comprehension," *Scientific Studies of Reading*, 22 (5): 384–400.

Mohamed, A. A. (2018), "Exposure Frequency in L2 Reading: An Eye-Movement Perspective of Incidental Vocabulary Learning," *Studies in Second Language Acquisition*, 40: 269–93.

Mokhtari, K. and C. Reichard (2002), "Assessing Students' Metacognitive Awareness of Reading Strategies," *Journal of Educational Psychology*, 94 (2): 249–59.

Mokhtari, K. and C. Reichard (2004), "Investigating the Strategic Reading Processes of First and Second Language Readers in Two Different Cultural Contexts," *System*, 32: 379–94.

Mondria, J.-A. (2003), "The Effects of Inferring, Verifying, and Memorizing on the Retention of L2 Word Meanings," *Studies in Second Language Acquisition*, 25: 473–99.

Montrul, S. (2001), "Agentive Verbs of Manner of Motion in Spanish and English as Second Languages," *Studies in Second Language Acquisition*, 23: 171–206.

Morett, L. M. and B. MacWhinney (2013), "Syntactic Transfer in English-Speaking Spanish Learners," *Bilingualism: Language and Cognition*, 16 (1): 132–51.

Mori, Y. and W. Nagy (1999), "Integration of Information from Context and Word Elements in Interpreting Novel Kanji Compounds," *Reading Research Quarterly*, 34: 80–101.

Mulder, E., M. van de Ven, E. Segers and L. Verhoeven (2019), "Context, Word, and Student Predictors in Second Language Vocabulary Learning," *Applied Psycholinguistics*, 40: 137–66.

Muljani, D., K. Koda and D. R. Moates (1998), "The Development of Word Recognition in a Second Language," *Applied Psycholinguistics*, 19: 99–113.

Nagy, W. E. (1997), "On the Role of Context in First- and Second-Language Vocabulary Learning," in N. Schmitt and M. McCarthy (eds.), *Vocabulary: Description, Acquisition, and Pedagogy*, 64–83, Cambridge: Cambridge University Press.

Nagy, W. E. and R. C. Anderson (1984), "How Many Words Are There in Printed School English? *Reading Research Quarterly*, 19 (3): 304–30.

Nagy, W. E., P. A. Herman and R. C. Anderson (1985), "Learning Words from Context," *Reading Research Quarterly*, 20: 233–53.

Nagy, W. E., R. C. Anderson and P. A. Herman (1987), "Learning Word Meanings from Context during Normal Reading," *American Educational Research Journal*, 24: 237–70.

Nagy, W. E. and P. A. Herman (1987), "Breadth and Depth of Vocabulary Knowledge: Implications for Acquisition and Instruction," in M. G. McKeown and M. E. Curtis (eds.), *The Nature of Vocabulary Acquisition*, 19–36, Hillsdale: Lawrence Erlbaum.

Nakanishi, T. (2015), "A Meta-Analysis of Extensive Reading Research," *TESOL Quarterly*, 49 (1): 6–37.

Nassaji, H. (2003a), "L2 Vocabulary Learning from Context: Strategies, Knowledge Sources, and Their Relationship with Success in L2 Lexical Inferencing," *TESOL Quarterly*, 37: 645–70.

Nassaji, H. (2003b), "Higher-Level and Lower-Level Text Processing Skills in Advanced ESL Reading Comprehension," *The Modern Language Journal*, 87 (2): 261–76.

Nation, I. S. P. (2001), *Learning Vocabulary in Another Language*, Cambridge: Cambridge University Press.

Nation, I. S. P. (2006), "How Large a Vocabulary Is Needed for Reading and Listening?," *The Canadian Modern Language Review*, 63 (1): 59–82.

Nation, I. S. P. and R. Waring (2020), *Teaching Extensive Reading in Another Language*, New York: Routledge.

Nation, K. and J. Cocksey (2009), "Beginning Readers Activate Semantics from Sub-Word Orthography," *Cognition*, 110: 273–8.

Nation, P. (2015), "Principles Guiding Vocabulary Learning through Extensive Reading," *Reading in a Foreign Language*, 27 (1): 136–45.

Nation, P. and K. M.-T. Wang (1999), "Graded Readers and Vocabulary," *Reading in a Foreign Language*, 12 (2): 355–80.

Nicoladis, E. (1999), " 'Where is My Brush-Teeth?' Acquisition of Compound Nouns in a French-English Bilingual Child," *Bilingualism: Language and Cognition*, 2 (3): 245–56.

Nicoladis, E. (2002), "What's the Difference between 'Toilet Paper' and 'Paper Toilet'? French-English Bilingual Children's Crosslinguistic Transfer in Compound Nouns," *Journal of Child Language*, 29: 843–63.

Nunes, T., P. Bryant and M. Bindman (2006), "The Effects of Learning to Spell on Children's Awareness of Morphology," *Reading and Writing*, 19 (7): 767–87.

Oakhill, J. and A. Garnham (1992), "Linguistic Prescriptions and Anaphoric Reality," *Text and Talk*, 12 (2): 161–82.

Ogle, D. M. (1986), "K-W-L: A Teaching Model that Develops Active Reading of Expository Text," *The Reading Teacher*, 39 (6): 564–70.

Olson, R. K., H. Forsberg and B. Wise (1994), "Genes, Environment, and the Development of Orthographic Skills," in V. W. Berninger (ed.), *The Varieties of Orthographic Knowledge I: Theoretical and Developmental Issues*, 27–71, Dordrecht: Kluwer Academic Publishers.

Omaki, A. and B. Schulz (2011), "Filler-Gap Dependencies and Island Constraints in Second-Language Sentence Processing," *Studies in Second Language Acquisition*, 33: 563–88.

O'Malley, J., A. Chamot, G. Stewner-Manzanares, R. Russo and L. Kupper (1985), "Learning Strategy Applications with Students of English as a Second Language," *TESOL Quarterly*, 19: 557–84.

Ota, M., R. J. Hartsuiker and S. L. Haywood (2009), "The KEY to the ROCK: Near-Homophony in Nonnative Visual Word Recognition," *Cognition*, 111: 263–9.

Ota, M., R. J. Hartsuiker and S. L. Haywood (2010), "Is a FAN Always FUN? Phonological and Orthographic Effects in Bilingual Visual Word Recognition," *Language and Speech*, 53 (3): 383–403.

Pagán, A and K. Nation (2019), "Learning Words via Reading: Contextual Diversity, Spacing, and Retrieval Effects in Adults," *Cognitive Science*, 43: e12705.

Palincsar, A. S. and A. L. Brown (1984), "Reciprocal Teaching of Comprehension-Monitoring Activities," *Cognition and Instruction*, 1 (2): 117–75.

Papagno, C., T. Valentine and A. Baddeley (1991), "Phonological Short-Term Memory and Foreign-Language Vocabulary Learning," *Journal of Memory and Language*, 30: 331–47.

Paribakht, T. S. (2005), "The Influence of First Language Lexicalization on Second Language Lexical Inferencing: A Study of Farsi-Speaking Learners of English as a Foreign Language," *Language Learning*, 55: 701–48.

Paribakht, T. S. and M.-C. Tréville (2007), "Lexical Inference among French Speakers and Persian Speakers When Reading English Texts: Effect of Lexicalization in First language," *The Canadian Modern Language Review*, 63 (3): 399–428.

Paribakht, T. S. and M. Wesche (1996), "Enhancing Vocabulary Acquisition through Reading: A Hierarchy of Text-Related Exercise Types," *The Canadian Modern Language Review*, 52 (2): 155–73.

Paribakht, T. S. and M. Wesche (1999), "Reading and 'Incidental' L2 Vocabulary Acquisition: An Introspective Study of Lexical Inferencing," *Studies in Second Language Acquisition*, 21: 195–224.

Pasquarella, A., X. Chen, K. Lam, Y. C. Luo and G. Ramirez (2011), "Cross-Language Transfer of Morphological Awareness in Chinese-English Bilinguals," *Journal of Research in Reading*, 34 (1): 23–42.

Pasquarella, A., X. Chen, A. Gottardo and E. Geva (2015), "Cross-Language Transfer of Word Reading Accuracy and Word Reading Fluency in Spanish-English and Chinese-English Bilinguals: Script-Universal and Script-Specific Processes," *Journal of Educational Psychology*, 107 (1): 96–110.

Pearson, P. D. and R. J. Spiro (1980), "Toward a Theory of Reading Comprehension Instruction," *Topics in Language Disorders*, 1 (1): 71–88.

Pellicer-Sánchez, A. (2016), "Incidental L2 Vocabulary Acquisition from and while Reading: An Eye-Tracking Study," *Studies in Second Language Acquisition*, 38: 97–130.

Pellicer-Sánchez, A. and N. Schmitt (2010), "Incidental Vocabulary Acquisition from an Authentic Novel: Do *Things Fall Apart*?," *Reading in a Foreign Language*, 22 (1): 31–55.

Perfetti, C. A. (1985), *Reading Ability*, New York: Oxford University Press.

Perfetti, C. A. (2003), "The Universal Grammar of Reading," *Scientific Studies of Reading*, 7 (1): 3–24.

Perfetti, C. A. (2007), "Reading Ability: Lexical Quality to Comprehension," *Scientific Studies of Reading*, 11 (4): 357–83.

Perfetti, C. A. and L. Hart (2002), "The Lexical Quality Hypothesis," in L. Vehoeven, C. Elbro, and P. Reitsma (eds.), *Precursors of Functional Literacy*, 189–213, Amsterdam: John Benjamins.

Perfetti, C. A., Y. Liu and L. H. Tan (2005), "The Lexical Constituency Model: Some Implications of Research on Chinese for General Theories of Reading," *Psychological Review*, 112 (1): 43–59.

Perfetti, C. A. and S. Dunlap (2008), "Learning to Read: General Principles and Writing System Variations," in K. Koda and A. Zehler (eds.), *Learning to Read across Languages*, 13–38, Mahwah: Erlbaum.

Perry, C. and J. C. Ziegler (2007), "Nested Incremental Modeling in the Development of Computational Theories: The CDP+ Model of Reading Aloud," *Psychological Review*, 114 (2): 273–315.

Peters, E. (2012), "The Differential Effects of Two Vocabulary Instruction Methods on EFL Word Learning: A Study into Task Effectiveness," *IRAL*, 50: 213–38.

Peters, E., J. H. Hulstijn, L. Sercu and M. Lutjeharms (2009), "Learning L2 German Vocabulary through Reading: The Effect of Three Enhancement Techniques Compared," *Language Learning*, 59 (1): 113–51.

Picarello, K. (1986), "Classroom Management: Drop Everything and Read!," *The Reading Teacher*, 39 (8): 871–2.

Pichette, F., L. de Serres and M. Lafontaine (2012), "Sentence Reading and Writing for Second Language Vocabulary Acquisition," *Applied Linguistics*, 33 (1): 66–82.

Pigada, M. and N. Schmitt (2006), "Vocabulary Acquisition from Extensive Reading: A Case Study," *Reading in a Foreign Language*, 18 (1): 1–28.

Pilgreen, J. L. (2000), *The SSR Handbook: How to Organize and Manage a Sustained Silent Reading Program*, Portsmouth: Heinemann.

Pitts, M., H. White and S. Krashen (1989), "Acquiring Second Language Vocabulary through Reading: A Replication of the Clockwork Orange Study Using Second Language Learners," *Reading in a Foreign Language*, 5 (2): 271–5.

Prior, A., A. Goldina, M. Shany, E. Geva and T. Katzir (2014), "Lexical Inference in L2: Predictive Roles of Vocabulary Knowledge and Reading Skill Beyond Reading Comprehension," *Reading and Writing*, 27: 1467–84.

Proctor, C. P., M. Carlo, D. August and C. Snow (2005), "Native Spanish-Speaking Children Reading in English: Toward a Model of Comprehension," *Journal of Educational Psychology*, 97 (2): 246–56.

Pulido, D. (2003), "Modeling the Role of Second Language Proficiency and Topic Familiarity in Second Language Incidental Vocabulary Acquisition through Reading," *Language Learning*, 53 (2): 233–84.

Pulido, D. (2007), "The Effects of Topic Familiarity and Passage Sight Vocabulary on L2 Lexical Inferencing and Retention through Reading," *Applied Linguistics*, 28 (1): 66–86.

Pulido, D. (2009), "How Involved Are American L2 Leaners of Spanish in Lexical Input Processing Tasks during Reading?," *Studies in Second Language Acquisition*, 31: 31–58.

Pulido, D. and D. Z. Hambrick (2008), "The *Virtuous* Circle: Modeling Individual Differences in L2 Reading and Vocabulary Development," *Reading in a Foreign Language*, 20 (2): 164–90.

Qian, D. D. (1996), "ESL Vocabulary Acquisition: Contextualization and Decontextualization," *The Canadian Modern Language Review*, 53 (1): 120–42.

Ramirez, G., X. Chen, E. Giva and Y. Luo (2011), "Morphological Awareness and Word Reading in English Language Learners: Evidence from Spanish- and Chinese-Speaking Children," *Applied Psycholinguistics*, 32: 601–18.

Rance-Roney, J. (2010), "Jump-Starting Language and Schema for English-Language Learners: Teacher-Composed Digital Jumpstarts for Academic Reading," *Journal of Adolescent and Adult Literacy*, 53 (5): 386–95.

Randall, M. and P. Meara (1988), "How Arabs Read Roman Letters," *Reading in a Foreign Language*, 4: 133–45.

Reed, D. K. (2013), "The Effects of Explicit Instruction on the Reading Performance of Adolescent English Language Learners with Intellectual Disabilities," *TESOL Quarterly*, 47 (4): 743–760.

Rodrigo, V., D. Greenberg and D. Segal (2014), "Changes in Reading Habits by Low Literate Adults through Extensive Reading," *Reading in a Foreign Language*, 26 (1), 73–91.

Roehling, J. V., M. Hebert, J. R. Nelson and J. J. Bohaty (2017), "Text Structure Strategies for Improving Expository Reading Comprehension," *The Reading Teacher*, 71 (1): 71–82.

Rott, S. (1999), "The Effect of Exposure Frequency on Intermediate Language Learners' Incidental Vocabulary Acquisition and Retention through Reading," *Studies in Second Language Acquisition*, 21: 589–619.

Rott, S. (2005), "Processing Glosses: A Qualitative Exploration of How Form-Meaning Connections Are Established and Strengthened," *Reading in a Foreign Language*, 17 (2): 95–124.

Rott, S. (2007), "The Effect of Frequency of Input-Enhancements on Word Learning and Text Comprehension," *Language Learning*, 57 (2): 165–99.

Rott, S. and J. Williams (2003), "Making Form-Meaning Connections while Reading: A Qualitative Analysis of Word Processing," *Reading in a Foreign Language*, 15 (1): 45–75.

Ryan, A. and P. Meara (1991), "The Case of Invisible Vowels: Arabic Speakers Reading English Words," *Reading in a Foreign Language*, 7: 531–40.

Saiegh-Haddad, E. and E. Geva (2008), "Morphological Awareness, Phonological Awareness, and Reading in English-Arabic Bilingual Children," *Reading and Writing*, 21: 481–504.

Saigh, K. and N. Schmitt (2012), "Difficulties with Vocabulary Word Form: The Case of Arabic ESL Learners," *System*, 40: 24–36.

Salataci R. and A. Akyel (2002), "Possible Effects of Strategy Instruction on L1 and L2 Reading," *Reading in a Foreign Language*, 14 (1): 1–17.

Sandra, D. (1990), "On the Representation and Processing of Compound Words: Automatic Access to Constituent Morphemes Does Not Occur," *The Quarterly Journal of Experimental Psychology*, 42A (3): 529–67.

Saragi, T., I. S. P. Nation and G. F. Meister (1978), "Vocabulary Learning and Reading," *System*, 6 (2): 72–8.

Sasaki, Y. (1991), "English and Japanese Interlanguage Comprehension Strategies: An Analysis Based on the Competition Model," *Applied Psycholinguistics*, 12: 47–73.

Schmidt, R. (1994), "Deconstructing Consciousness in Search of Useful Definitions for Applied Linguistics," *AILA Review*, 11: 11–26.

Schoonen, R., J. Hulstijn and B. Bossers (1998), "Metacognitive and Language-specific Knowledge in Native and Foreign Language Reading Comprehension: An Empirical Study among Dutch Students in Grades 6, 8 and 10," *Language Learning*, 48 (1): 71–106.

Segalowitz, N. (2003), "Automaticity and Second Languages," in C. Doughty and M. Long (eds.), *The Handbook of Second Language Acquisition*, 382–408, Malden: Blackwell.

Seidenberg, M. S. and J. L. McClelland (1989), "A Distributed, Developmental Model of Word Recognition," *Psychological Review*, 96: 523–68.

Selkirk, E. (1982), *The Syntax of Words*, Cambridge, MA: MIT Press.

Senoo, Y. and K. Yonemoto (2014), "Vocabulary Learning through Extensive Reading: A Case Study," *The Canadian Journal of Applied Linguistics*, 17 (2): 1–22.

Service, E. and V. Kohonen (1995), "Is the Relation between Phonological Memory and Foreign Language Learning Accounted for by Vocabulary Acquisition?," *Applied Psycholinguistics*, 16: 155–72.

Shafiro, V. and A. V. Kharkhurin (2009), "The Role of Native-Language Phonology in the Auditory Word Identification and Visual Word Recognition of Russian-English bilinguals," *Journal of Psycholinguistic Research*, 38: 93–110.

Sharp, A. (2002), "Chinese L1 Schoolchildren Reading in English: The Effects of Rhetorical Patterns," *Reading in a Foreign Language*, 14 (2): 111–35.

Shore, W. J. and V. Kempe (1999), "The Role of Sentence Context in Accessing Partial Knowledge of Word Meanings," *Journal of Psycholinguistics Research*, 28 (2): 145–63.

Shu, H., R. C. Anderson and H. Zhang (1995), "Incidental Learning of Word Meanings while Reading: A Chinese and American Cross-Cultural Study," *Reading Research Quarterly*, 30 (1): 76–95.

Silva, R. and H. Clahsen (2008), "Morphologically Complex Words in L1 and L2 Processing: Evidence from Masked Priming Experiments in English," *Bilingualism: Language and Cognition*, 11: 245–60.

Skinner, B. E. (1957), *Verbal Behavior*, New York: Appleton-Century-Crofts.

Slobin, D. I. (1970), "Universals of Grammatical Development in Children," in G. B. Flores d'Arcais and W. J. M. Levelt (eds.), *Advances in Psycholinguistics*, 174–86, Amsterdam: North-Holland Publishing.

Sorace, A. (2011), "Pinning down the Concept of 'Interface' in Bilingualism," *Linguistics Approaches to Bilingualism*, 1: 1–33.

Sorace, A. and F. Filiaci (2006), "Anaphora Resolution in Near-Native Speakers of Italian," *Second Language Research*, 22 (3): 339–68.

Sparks, R. L. (2015), "Language Deficits in Poor L2 Comprehends: The Simple View," *Foreign Language Annals*, 48 (4): 635–58.

Sparks, R. L., J. Patton, L. Ganschow and N. Humbach (2012), "Do L1 Reading Achievement and L1 Print Exposure Contribute to the Prediction of L2 Proficiency?," *Language Learning*, 62 (2): 473–505.

Stahl, S. A. (1992), "Saying the 'P' Word: Nine Guidelines for Exemplary Phonics Instruction," *The Reading Teacher*, 45 (8): 618–25.

Stahl, S. A. (2004), "What Do We Know About Fluency? Findings of the National Reading Panel," in P. McCardle and V. Chhabra (eds.), *The Voice of Evidence in Reading Research*, 187–211, Baltimore: Brookes Publishing.

Stanovich, K. E. (1984), "The Interactive-Compensatory Model of Reading: A Confluence of Developmental, Experimental, and Educational Psychology," *RASE: Remedial and Special Education*, 5 (3): 11–19.

Stanovich, K. E., R. F. West and D. J. Feeman (1981), "A Longitudinal Study of Sentence Context Effects in Second-Grade Children: Tests of an Interactive-Compensatory Model," *Journal of Experimental Child Psychology*, 32: 185–99.

Sternberg, R. J. (1987), "Most Vocabulary is Learned from Context," in M. G. McKeown and M. E. Curtis (eds.), *The Nature of Vocabulary Acquisition*, 89–105, Hillsdale: Lawrence Erlbaum.

Sternberg, R. J. and J. S. Powell (1983), "Comprehending Verbal Comprehension," *American Psychologist*, 38 (8): 878–93.

Stewart, A. J., M. J. Pickering and A. J. Sanford (2000), "The Time Course of the Influence of Implicit Causality Information: Focusing versus Integration Accounts," *Journal of Memory and Language*, 42: 423–43.

Stoller, F. L. (2015), "Viewing Extensive Reading from Different Vantage Points," *Reading in a Foreign Language*, 27 (1), 152–9.

Stroop, J. R. (1935), "Studies of Interference in Serial Verbal Reactions," *Journal of Experimental Psychology*, 18 (6): 643–62.

Su, I.-R. (2001), "Transfer of Sentence Processing Strategies: A Comparison of L2 Learners of Chinese and English," *Applied Psycholinguistics*, 22: 83–112.

Su, I.-R. (2004), "The Effects of Discourse Processing with Regard to Syntactic and Semantic Cues: A Competition Model Study," *Applied Psycholinguistics*, 25: 587–601.

Suk, H. (2016), "The Effects of Extensive Reading on Reading Comprehension, Reading Rate, and Vocabulary Acquisition," *Reading Research Quarterly*, 52 (1): 73–89.

Sun, C.-H. (2017), "The Value of Picture-Book Reading-Based Collaborative Output Activities for Vocabulary Retention," *Language Teaching Research*, 21 (1): 96–117.

Swanborn, M. S. L. and K. de Glopper (1999), "Incidental Word Learning while Reading: A Meta-Analysis," *Review of Educational Research*, 69 (3): 261–85.

Sylvester, R. and W.-I. Greenidge (2009), "Digital Storytelling: Extending the Potential for Struggling Writers," *The Reading Teacher*, 63 (4): 284–95.

Taguchi, E., M. Takayasu-Maass and G. J. Gorsuch (2004), "Developing Reading Fluency in EFL: How Assisted Repeated Reading and Extensive Reading Affect Fluency Development," *Reading in a Foreign Language*, 16 (2): 70–96.

Tian, G. H. (1990), "The Effects of Rhetorical Organization in Expository Prose on ESL Readers in Singapore," *RELC Journal*, 21 (2): 1–13.

Tibi, S. and J. R. Kirby (2018), "Investigating Phonological Awareness and Naming Speed as Predictors of Reading in Arabic," *Scientific Studies of Reading*, 22 (1): 70–84.

Tilstra, J., K. McMaster, P. van den Broek, P. Kendeou and D. Rapp (2009), "Simple but Complex: Components of the Simple View of Reading across Grade Levels," *Journal of Research in Reading*, 32 (4): 383–401.

Torgesen, J. K., S. T. Morgan and C. Davis (1992), "Effects of Two Types of Phonological Awareness Training on Word Learning in Kindergarten Children," *Journal of Educational Psychology*, 84 (3): 364–70.

Tremblay, A. (2008), "Is Second Language Lexical access Prosodically Constrained? Processing of Word Stress by French Canadian Second Language Learners of English," *Applied Psycholinguistics*, 29: 553–84.

Türk, E. and G. Erçetin (2014), "Effects of Interactive Versus Simultaneous Display of Multimedia Glosses on L2 Reading Comprehension and Incidental Vocabulary Learning," *Computer Assisted Language Learning*, 27 (1): 1–25.

Underwood, G. and V. Batt (1996), *Reading and Understanding*, Malden: Blackwell.

Vainio, S., A. Pajunen and J. Hyönä (2014), "L1 and L2 Word Recognition in Finnish: Examining L1 Effects on L2 Processing of Morphological Complexity and Morphophonological Transparency," *Studies in Second Language Acquisition*, 36: 133–62.

van Dijk, T. A. and W. Kintsch (1983), *Strategies of Discourse Comprehension*, New York: Academic Press.

van Orden, G. C. (1987), "A ROWS is a ROSE: Spelling, Sound, and Reading," *Memory and Cognition*, 15 (3): 181–98.

Verhoeven, L. (1994), "Transfer in Bilingual Development: The Linguistic Interdependency Hypothesis Revisited," *Language Learning*, 44: 381–415.

Verhoeven, L. and J. van Leeuwe (2008), "Prediction of the Development of Reading Comprehension: A Longitudinal Study," *Applied Cognitive Psychology*, 22: 407–23.

Verhoeven, L. and J. van Leeuwe (2012), "The Simple View of Second Language Reading throughout the Primary Grades," *Reading and Writing*, 25: 1805–18.

Verhoeven, L. and C. A. Perfetti (2011), "Morphological Processing in Reading Acquisition: A Cross-Linguistic Perspective," *Applied Psycholinguistics*, 32: 457–66.

Verhoeven, L., J. van Leeuwe and A. Vermeer (2011), "Vocabulary Growth and Reading Development across the Elementary School Years," *Scientific Studies of Reading*, 15 (1): 8–25.

Wade-Woolley, L. and E. Geva (2000), "Processing Novel Phonemic Contrasts in the Acquisition of L2 Word Reading," *Scientific Studies of Reading*, 4 (4): 295–311.

Wagner, R. K. and J. K. Torgesen (1987), "The Nature of Phonological Processing and Its Causal Role in the Acquisition of Reading Skills," *Psychological Bulletin*, 101 (2): 192–212.

Wagner, R. K., J. K. Torgesen, C. A. Rashotte and N. A. Pearson (2010), *Test of Silent Reading Efficiency and Comprehension*, Austin: Pro-Ed.

Walter, C. (2004), "Transfer of Reading Comprehension Skills to L2 is Linked to Mental Representations of Text and to L2 Working Memory," *Applied Linguistics*, 25 (3): 315–39.

Wang, M., K. Koda and C. A. Perfetti (2003), "Alphabetic and Nonalphabetic L1 Effects in English Word Identification: A Comparison of Korean and Chinese English L2 Learners," *Cognition*, 87: 129–49.

Wang, M. and K. Koda (2005), "Commonalities and Differences in Word Identification Skills among Learners of English as a Second Language," *Language Learning*, 55: 71–98.

Waring, R. and M. Takaki (2003), "At What Rate Do Learners Learn and Retain New Vocabulary from Reading a Graded Reader?," *Reading in a Foreign Language*, 15 (2): 130–63.

Watanabe, Y. (1997), "Input, Intake, and Retention: Effects of Increased Processing on Incidental Learning of Foreign Language Vocabulary," *Studies in Second Language Acquisition*, 19: 287–307.

Weaver, P. A. (1979), "Improving Reading Comprehension: Effects of Sentence Organization Instruction," *Reading Research Quarterly*, 15 (1): 129–46.

Webb, S. (2007a), "The Effects of Synonymy on Second-Language Vocabulary Learning," *Reading in a Foreign Language*, 19: 120–36.

Webb, S. (2007b), "The Effects of Repetition on Vocabulary Knowledge," *Applied Linguistics*, 28 (1): 46–65.

Webb, S. and A. C.-S. Chang (2012), "Vocabulary Learning through Assisted and Unassisted Repeated Reading," *The Canadian Modern Language Review*, 68 (3): 267–90.

Webb, S. and A. C.-S. Chang (2015a), "How Does Prior Word Knowledge Affect Vocabulary Learning Progress in an Extensive Reading Program?," *Studies in Second Language Acquisition*, 37: 651–75.

Webb, S. and A. C.-S. Chang (2015b), "Second Language Vocabulary Learning through Extensive Reading with Audio Support: How Do Frequency and Distribution of Occurrence Affect Learning?," *Language Teaching Research*, 19 (6): 667–86.

Webb, S. and P. Nation (2017), *How Vocabulary Is Learned*, Oxford: Oxford University Press.

Wesche, M. B. and T. S. Paribakht (1996), "Assessing Second Language Vocabulary Knowledge: Depth Versus Breadth," *The Canadian Modern Language Review*, 53 (1): 13–40.

Wesche, M. B. and T. S. Paribakht (2010), *Lexical Inferencing in a First and Second Language: Cross-Linguistic Dimensions*, Bristol: Multilingual Matters.

Wimmer, H., K. Landerl, R. Linortner and P. Hummer (1991), "The Relationship of Phonemic Awareness to Reading Acquisition: More Consequence Than Precondition but Still Important," *Cognition*, 40: 219–49.

Witzel, J., N. Witzel and J. Nicol (2012), "Deeper Than Shallow: Evidence for Structure-Based Parsing Biases in Second-Language Sentence Processing," *Applied Psycholinguistics*, 33: 419–56.

Wolf, M. (2007), *Proust and the Squid: The Story and Science of the Reading Brain*, New York: Harper.

Wong, Y. K. (2017), "Relationship between Reading Comprehension and Its Components in Young Chinese-as-a-Second-Language Learners," *Reading and Writing*, 30: 969–88.

Woodcock, R. W. (1987), *Woodcock Reading Mastery Tests-Revised*, Circle Pines: American Guidance Service.

Yamashita, J. (2002), "Mutual Compensation between L1 Reading Ability and L2 Language Proficiency in L2 Reading Comprehension," *Journal of Research in Reading*, 25 (1): 81–95.

Yamashita, J. (2015), "In Search of the Nature of Extensive Reading in L2: Cognitive, Affective, and Pedagogical Perspectives," *Reading in a Foreign Language*, 29 (1): 168–81.

Yorio, C. A. (1971), "Some Sources of Reading Problems in Foreign Language Learners," *Language Learning*, 21: 107–15.

Yoshii, M. and J. Flaitz (2002), "Second Language Incidental Vocabulary Retention: The Effect of Text and Picture Annotation Types," *CALICO Journal*, 20 (1): 33–58.

Yoshimura, Y. and B. MacWhinney (2010), "The Use of Pronominal Case in English Sentence Interpretation," *Applied Psycholinguistics*, 31: 619–33.

Zagar, D., J. Pynte and S. Rativeau (1997), "Evidence for Early Closure Attachment on First-Pass Reading Times in French," *Quarterly Journal of Experimental Psychology*, 50A: 421–38.

Zahar, R., T. Cobb and N. Spada (2001), "Acquiring Vocabulary through Reading: Effects of Frequency and Contextual Richness," *The Canadian Modern Language Review*, 57 (4): 541–72.

Zareva, A. (2012), "Partial Word Knowledge: Frontier Words in the L2 Mental Lexicon," *International Review of Applied Linguistics in Language Teaching*, 50 (4): 277–301.

Zhang, J., R. C. Anderson, Q. Wang, J. Packard, X. Wu, S. Tang and X. Ke (2012), "Insight into the Structure of Compound Words among Speakers of Chinese and English," *Applied Psycholinguistics*, 33: 752–79.

Zhou, X. and V. Murphy (2011), "How English L2 Learners in China Perceive and Interpret Novel English Compounds," *Asian EFL Journal*, 13 (1): 329–56.

Ziegler, J. C. and U. Goswami (2005), "Reading Acquisition, Developmental Dyslexia, and Skilled Reading across Languages: A Psycholinguistic Grain Size Theory," *Psychological Bulletin*, 131: 3–29.

Ziegler, J. C. and U. Goswami (2006), "Becoming Literate in Different Languages: Similar Problems, Different Solutions," *Developmental Science*, 9: 429–53.

Zwaan, R. A. (1999), "Situation Models: The Mental Leap into Imagined Worlds," *Current Directions in Psychological Science*, 8 (1): 15–18.

Index

adorable 58
affluence 73
agent of sentence 100-1
agreement 101-2; *see also* subject-
 verb agreement
Akamatsu, N. 53, 114
Alderson, J. C. 51
Alhaqbani, A. 106-7
alphabetic principle 67
alphabetic writing system of
 language 65-6
Alptekin, C. 105
Anderson, R. C. 20, 80
assisted-repeated reading 40
audio-assisted reading 40
automaticity
 in L2 sentence processing 91-2
 in reading processes 47

Ballantyne, J. C. 102
Bamford, J. 9
bank 50
Barcroft, J. 26, 38
Bartolotti, J. 77
basic interpersonal communication
 skills (BICS) 52
Beck, I. L. 35
behavioristic approach, in learning 4-5
Bensoussan, M. 105
Berko, J. 112
Block, J. 17-18
book flood 8
bottom-up approaches, reading 98
Boustead, T. M. 111
Bowers, J. S. 73
Bransford, J. D. 96
Brown, R. 40
Bryant, P. 19

Cain, K. 19
Carr, T. H. 45
Carrell, P. L. 105-6, 118

Carruthers, J. 110
Carson, K. L. 111
Carton, A. 7
carwash 72
Chang, A. C.-S. 22, 40
Chen, C. 30
Chen, C.-L. A. 40
Chern, C.-L. 31, 34
Clarke, D. A. 121-2
Clarke, M. A. 51
Clifton, C., Jr. 89
Clockwork Orange, A (Burgess) 21
Coady, J. 6, 14, 29
Cobb, T. 21-2, 35, 36
cognates 32
cognitive academic language
 proficiency (CALP) 52
cognitive model of word-meaning
 inference 56-61
 contextual information 58
  dual processing of 59
  generation process 58-9,
   83-107
  reading comprehension 61
 instruction
  approaches in 120-2
  recommendations for 122-4
 metalinguistic awareness 108-9
  morphological awareness 112-13
  orthographic awareness 109-10
  phonological awareness 109
  programmatic approaches 110-11
 overview 56-7
 pedagogical applications 108-25
 reading, lower-level and higher-level
  processes in 59-60
 reading comprehension 61, 115-20
 word-form information 57
  dual processing of 59
  extraction 58
  word recognition processes 60-1
 word recognition processes 60-1

cognitive models of reading
    processes   45–51
  automaticity   47
  component skills approach   45–6
  information-processing
    approach   46–7
  interactive compensatory
    model   49–50
  lexical quality hypothesis   50–1
  simple view of reading   48–9
  working memory   47
cognitive processes, in learning   5, 19
collaborative strategic reading   119
component skills approach   45–6, 115–20
comprehension   61, 90, 93–8
  background knowledge, activating and
    supporting   117–18
  construction-integration model   96–7
  reading, promotion of   116–20
  schema theory   95–6
  sentence processing and interpretation,
    promotion of   115–16
  strategies   118–20
  text   93–5
  top-down/bottom-up/interactive
    approaches   97–8
connectionist model, word
    recognition   70–1
Conroy, M. A.   92
constraint-based models   89
construction-integration model   96–7
contextual helpfulness   34–5
contextual information   55–6, 58
  dual processing of   59
  generation process   58–9, 83–107
    cross-linguistic transfer
      during   98–107
    reading comprehension   93–8
    sentence   83–93
  reading comprehension   61, 93–8
contextual processing   18
Crain, S.   84, 89
crept   73
cross-linguistic approach/transfer   52–4
  contextual information,
    generation of   98–107
    agent of sentence,
      identification of   100–1
    discourse structure   105–6
    metacognitive strategies   106–7

    pronouns   103–4
    sensitivity to agreement   101–2
    sentence processing   98–100
    topic familiarity   104–5
    verb usage, structural
      difference in   102–3
  word-form information
    extraction   72–82, 98–107
    L1 phonological transfer   75–6
    morphological information   78–9
    orthographic/phonological
      information   74
    phonological and orthographic
      structures   76–7
    phonological processing   77–8
    phonological short-term
      memory   77–8
    semantically/morphologically
      unrelated letter string,
      misled by   73
    semantic transparency   80–2
    vowels   74–5
    written word   72–3
Cuetos, F.   99
Cunnings, I.   92
Cupples, L.   92
Cziko, G. A.   51

Daneman, M.   18–19
Davis, C. J.   73
Day, R. R.   9, 21
Deacon, S. H.   46, 110
de Bot, K.   17, 33
decay   30
decoding   48, 52–4; see also
    phonological decoding
default learning hypothesis; see incidental
    learning hypothesis
de Glopper, K.   20
de Leeuw, L.   37
de Serres, L.   29
dictionaries   38–9
digital storytelling technology   117–18
directed reading and thinking activity
    (DRTA)   119
Dixon, R.   3–4
Donkaewbua, S.   40
Drop Everything And Read (DEAR)   8
dual route model, word
    recognition   69–70

Dupuy, B. 21
Dupuy, H. 4
Durso, F. T. 13

Ehri, L. C. 67
Elley, W. B. 8–9
Erçetin, G. 38–9
Erwin, B. 117
experience-text-relationship (ETR) approach 118
extensive reading 8–9, 21–2
extra-lingual cues 7

Fender, M. 99
Ferreira, F. 89
Filiaci, F. 93
Flaitz, J. 38
fluency, reading/word recognition 8–9, 40, 48, 53, 85, 108, 111, 113–15, 124–5
form-focused tasks 39–40
Foroodi-Nejad, F. 79
Forsberg, H. 110
Frantzen, D. 35
Fraser, C. A. 14
free voluntary reading 8
frequency of encounters 36–7
Fukkink, R. G. 115

garden path model 87–9
Garnham, A. 90
gend 7
Geva, E. 53
Gillon, G. T. 111
global cues 34–5
glosses 38–9
Goetz, E. T. 49
Goldsmith-Phillips, J. 49–50
Gor, J. 80
Gottardo, A. 116
Gough, P. B. 67
Grabe, W. 97–8, 120
grain size theory 68
grapheme-phoneme correspondences 67, 70, 110
graphic organizers 120
Green, D. 72
Green, I. 19
Greenidge, W.-I. 117–18

Haastrup, K. 7, 16–17

habitat 73
Hamada, M. 19, 31, 73–4, 78
Hambrick, D. Z. 14
Han, A. 40
Hanley, D. A. 73
Hardy, Tomas 21
Harrington, M. 116
Hartsuiker, R. J. 75–6
Hayes-Harb, R. 75
Haynes, M. 73
Haywood, S. L. 75–6
Herman, P. A. 12, 20
Hiramatsu, M. 21
Hirsh, D. 29
hogwash 72
Holmes, V. M. 110
Horst, M. 21–2, 36
Hu, H.-C. M. 33
Huckin, T. 6, 17–18
Hulstijn, J. H. 6, 25, 115–16
Hyönä, J. 78

Inagaki, S. 102
incidental learning 6
incidental learning hypothesis 3, 9–10
    origin 3–4
    in second language
        incidental word learning 5–7
        lexical inference 7–8
        reading instruction 8–9
        theoretical background 4–5
incidental word learning 5–8, 21–2
independent reading 8
inferencing 7; *see also* lexical inference
information-processing approach 46–7
input processing 15–16
intentional learning 6
interactive approaches, reading 98
interactive compensatory model 49–50
interface hypothesis 93
inter-lingual cues 7
intra-lingual cues 7

Jegerski, J. 103
Jenkins, J. R. 3–4, 110
Jiang, N. 80, 101–2, 120
Joe, A. 37
Johnson, M. K. 96
Juel, C. 67
Juffs, A. 103, 116

Kaan, E.   102
Kaplan, R. B.   105
Keating, G. D.   103
Kern, R. G.   34
Kim, H.-R.   36
Kim, Y. H.   49
Kirby, J. R.   46
Klinger, J. K.   118
Knight, S.   24
knowledge sources/strategies   32-4
known words   54-5
Koda, K.   19, 52, 73-4, 76, 78, 84, 112
Konopak, K.   23
Krashen, S.   5, 21
Krashen's hypotheses   5
Kucan, L.   111
Kweon, S.-O.   36
K-W-L approach   118

L1 reading ability   52
L2 learners, earlier studies
    with   20-1
L2 reading, theories in   51-4
    cross-linguistic approach   52-4
    L1 reading ability   52
    proficiency   51-2
L2 sentence processing/interpretation
    processing capacity   91-2
    syntactic processing,
        development of   92-3
Lafontaine, M.   29
language(s)   5, 63-4
    oral   64-5
    written   64-5
Laufer, B.   6, 26, 29, 39
Levelt's speech production model   17
Levy, B. A.   45
lexical inference   7-8
    definition   7
    extra-lingual cues in   7
    inter-lingual cues in   7
    intra-lingual cues in   7
lexical processing model   17
lexical quality hypothesis   50-1
lexical representations   50
Li, M.   80
linguistic factors/strategies, word learning
    from reading
    knowledge sources and
        strategies   32-4
    known word coverage   28-9

morphological factors   30-1
orthographic factors   32
semantic factors   29-30
vocabulary knowledge   28-9
Liu, N.   29
local cues   34
Logan, B.   30-1
logographic writing system of
    language   66, 68-9
low   50

McCaslin, E. S.   35
McClelland, J. L.   70
McCutchen, D.   30-1
McKeown, M. G.   35
McKoon, G.   96
Mangubhai, F.   8-9
Marian, V.   77
Mayor of Casterbridge, The
    (Jones)   21-2
meaning-focused tasks   39-40
meaning-inferred *vs.* meaning-given
    methods   25-6
Meara, P.   72, 75
Meara, T.   21-2, 36
Meister, G. F.   21
mental representation   94
metacognitive awareness of reading
    strategies inventory
    (MARSI)   106
metalinguistic awareness   108-9
    morphological awareness   112-13
    orthographic awareness   109-10
    phonological awareness   109
    programmatic approaches   110-11
Mimeau, C.   110
Mitchell, D. C.   99
Moates, D. R.   76
Mohamed, A. A.   36
Mokhtari, K.   106
Mondria, J.-A.   26
monitor model   5
Montrul, S.   103
Mori, Y.   31
morphological awareness   46, 53
morphological information   57,
    60-1, 78-9
Muljani, D.   76

Nagy, W. E.   12, 20, 31, 80
Nassaji, H.   23, 33, 46, 73, 110

Nation, I. S. P.   9, 12, 21, 29, 36, 56–7, 121–2
Nation, P.   29
native-speaking children, earlier studies with   19–20
Nicol, J.   104
Nicoladis, E.   79
nouns   7, 30, 54, 79, 84, 86, 89, 91, 99–101, 113

Oakhill, J.   19, 90
observe/observable/observation   28–9
Olson, R. K.   110
Omura, C.   21
orthographic depth   66–7
orthographic information   60–1, 74
orthographic knowledge   32, 57
orthographic system   66–7
orthography   32
Ota, M.   75–6

Pagán, A.   36
Pajunen, A.   78
Paradis, J.   79
Paribakht, T. S.   15–17, 30, 32–4
partial word knowledge   13
Pearson, P. D.   117
Pellicer-Sánchez, A.   36
Perfetti, C. A.   72, 74
permeated   73
phonics   110–11
phonological awareness   46, 53
phonological decoding   60
phonological information   57, 60–1, 74
Pichette, F.   29
Pigada, M.   22
pigpen   54–6
Pitts, M.   20–1
pleasure reading   8
Powell, J. S.   18, 122
preposition   91
processing capacity   18–19
processing deficit hypothesis   84–5
proficiency   51–2
prognosis   30
pronouns   84, 86, 90–3, 102–4
propositions   96–7
pseudo-homophone   110
pseudowords   32, 48, 76–7, 110, 114
Pulido, D.   14, 23–4, 35

Qian, D. D.   26
questioning the author approach   119

Rance-Roney, J.   117
rapid automatic naming (RAN) task   114
Ratcliff, R.   96
reading; *see also* cognitive models of reading processes; L1 reading ability; L2 reading, theories in
   assisted-repeated   40
   audio-assisted   40
   automaticity in   47
   comprehension   61, 93–8
      construction-integration model   96–7
      schema theory   95–6
      text   93–5
      top-down/bottom-up/interactive approaches   97–8
   extensive   8–9, 21–2
   free voluntary   8
   higher-level processes in   60
   independent   8
   instruction   8–9
   lower-level processes in   59–60
   pleasure   8
   repeated   40
   simple view of   48–9
   span test   19
   top-down approach   69
reciprocal teaching   119
references   90
Reichard, C.   106
repeated reading   40
retention of words   23–5
Riazi, M.   106–7
Ricketts, J.   110
Rott, S.   36, 38
Rozovski-Roitblat, B.   39
Ryan, A.   75

Saiegh-Haddad, E.   53
Saigh, K.   75
Saragi, T.   21
SCANR instruction   120–1
schema theory   95–6
Schmidt, N.   75
Schmidt, R.   6
Schmitt, N.   22, 36
Schoonen, R.   116
Schumm, J. S.   118

second language, incidental learning hypothesis in
  incidental word learning 5–7
  lexical inference 7–8
  reading instruction 8–9
  theoretical background 4–5
Segers, E. 37
Seidenberg, M. S. 70
selective combination 18
selective comparison 18
selective encoding 18
Selkirk, E. 31
semantic information 60–1, 80–2
Senoo, Y. 22
sentence processing/interpretation 83–93
  anaphoric references and comprehension 90
  automaticity 91–2
  constraint-based models 89
  garden path model 87–9
  influencing factors 83–5
  L2
    processing capacity 91–2
    syntactic processing, development of 92–3
  shallow structure hypothesis 90–1
  syntactic knowledge in 84–5
  syntactic parsing 85–7
shallow structure hypothesis 90–1
Shankweiler, D. 84
Shore, W. J. 13
Shu, H. 20
Siegel, L. S. 116
Simis, A. 115
simple view of reading 48–9
slow 50
Sorace, A. 93
Spada, N. 35
Spiro, R. J. 117
spoken language 64–5
Stahl, S. A. 110–11
Stanovich, K. E. 116
Steedman, M. J. 89
Sternberg, R. J. 18, 122
structural deficit hypothesis 84–5
subject-verb agreement 101–2
Sun, C.-H. 37
sustained silent reading (SSR) 8
Swanborn, M. S. L. 20
swift 11–12

syllabic writing system of language 66
Sylvester, R. 117–18
syntactic knowledge 84–5
syntactic parsing 85–7

Takaki, M. 24
Test of Silent Reading Efficiency and Comprehension 115
think-aloud technique 118
top-down approach, reading 69, 97–8
topic familiarity 104–5
Tremblay, A. 77
Tréville, M.-C. 30
Trois hommes et un couffin 21
Truscott, J. 30
Türk, E. 38–9

unfamiliar words 14–15, 22–3, 54–5
unhappiness 30

Vainio, S. 78
van Gelderen, A. 116
van Leeuwe, J. 50–1
van Pattern, B. 103
Vaughn, S. 118
verb 84, 86–8, 92, 96, 99, 102–4
Verhoeven, L. 37, 50–2, 72
Vermeer, A. 50–1
visuals 117
vocabulary 4, 8–10, 13–15, 17, 21–2, 25, 28–9, 35, 40–1, 46, 48, 50–1, 53–5, 110–11, 115, 122–3
vocabulary knowledge scale 13
vowels 74–5

Waring, R. 9, 24, 40
Watanabe, Y. 38
Weaver, P. A. 116
Webb, S. 22, 30, 36, 40
Wesche, M. 15–16, 32–4
White, H. 21
Wijnen, F. 102
Wise, B. 110
Witzel, J. 104
Witzel, N. 104
Wolf, M. 64
word-form information 12, 57
  cross-linguistic transfer in 72–82
  dual processing of 59
  extraction 58, 63–82
  word recognition processes 60–1

word knowledge 56–7
  aspects 11–12
  breadth and depth 12–13
  definition 12
  development in reading 14
  frontier level 13
  known level 13
  partial 13
  unknown level 13
  vocabulary knowledge scale for 13
word learning from reading 11, 26–7
  contextual helpfulness in 34–5
  effectiveness
    incidental word learning during extensive reading 21–2
    L2 learners, earlier studies with 20–1
    meaning-inferred vs. meaning-given methods 25–6
    native-speaking children, earlier studies with 19–20
    retention of words 23–5
    unfamiliar words, attention to 22–3
  frameworks
    contextual processing 18
    input processing 15–16
    processing capacity 18–19
    unknown words during reading 14–15
    word-meaning inference processing 16–18
  frequency of encounters in 36–7
  linguistic factors and strategies in
    knowledge sources and strategies 32–4
    known word coverage 28–9
    morphological factors 30–1
    orthographic factors 32
    semantic factors 29–30
    vocabulary knowledge 28–9
  tasks and instruction 37–40
    audio-assisted reading 40
    dictionaries 38–9
    form-focused 39–40
    glosses 38–9
    meaning-focused 39–40
    repeated reading 40
  word knowledge
    aspects 11–12
    breadth and depth 12–13
    definition 12
    development in reading 14
    partial 13
word-meaning inference 8, 16–18
  cognitive model of 56–61
    contextual information 58–61
    overview 56–7
    pedagogical applications 108–25
    reading, lower-level and higher-level processes in 59–60
    reading comprehension 61
    word-form information 57–61
  instruction
    approaches in 120–2
    recommendations for 122–4
word recognition theories 63–72
  fluency in 111, 113–15, 124–5
  metalinguistic awareness 108–9
    morphological awareness 112–13
    orthographic awareness 109–10
    phonological awareness 109
    programmatic approaches 110–11
  models 69–72
  orthographic system 66–7
  in reading comprehension 69
  skills development 67–9
  spoken language 64–5
  writing system of language 65–6
  written language 63–5
words
  form 12
  information, use of 55–6
  meaning 12
  recognition 19, 46, 49, 60–1, 63–72
  retention of 23–5
  unfamiliar 14–15, 22–3
  use 12, 55
working memory 47, 77–8
writing system of language 65–6
  alphabetic 65–6
  logographic 66
  syllabic 66
written language 63–5

Yonemoto, K. 22
Yorio, C. A. 51
Yoshii, M. 38

Zahar, R. 35
Zhang, H. 20

www.ingramcontent.com/pod-product-compliance
Lightning Source LLC
Chambersburg PA
CBHW061840300426
44115CB00013B/2454